MANAGING
WORKPLACE
NEGATIVITY

MANAGING WORKPLACE NEGATIVITY

Gary S. Topchik

AMACOM
American Management Association

New York • Atlanta • Boston • Chicago • Kansas City • San Francisco • Washington, D. C.
Brussels • Mexico City • Tokyo • Toronto

Special discounts on bulk quantities of AMACOM books are available to corporations, professional associations, and other organizations. For details, contact Special Sales Department, AMACOM, a division of American Management Association, 1601 Broadway, New York, NY 10019.
Tel.: 212-903-8316.   Fax: 212-903-8083.
Web site: www.amacombooks.org

This publication is designed to provide accurate and authoritative information in regard to the subject matter covered. It is sold with the understanding that the publisher is not engaged in rendering legal, accounting, or other professional service. If legal advice or other expert assistance is required, the services of a competent professional person should be sought.

Library of Congress Cataloging-in-Publication Data

Topchik, Gary S.
    Managing workplace negativity/ Gary S. Topchik
        p.   cm.
    Includes index.
    ISBN 0-8144-0582-7
    1. Employee morale.   2. Employee motivation.   3. Supervision of employees.   4. Personnel management.   I. Title.   II. Author.
    HF5549.5.M6.T67   2000   00-44186
    658.3—dc 21   CIP

Printing number

10   9   8   7   6   5   4   3   2   1

CONTENTS

Introduction

Negativity is the eventual outcome of unchecked pessimism. It is a pattern of pessimistic thinking that persists over time. Individuals, teams, departments, or entire organizations can be pessimistic.

Negativity is spreading unchecked like a virus through many companies; it is causing productivity and morale problems. *Managing Workplace Negativity* tells you exactly what can be done to kill this virus. Negativity is expensive. It costs companies millions of dollars each year. Finding "cures" for the negativity virus will directly affect the success of today's organization. It is especially hard to remain competitive if the staff's work attitude is influencing productivity and morale.

Managing Workplace Negativity gives you very practical examples of how to turn around negative individuals, negative teams, and negative organizations. Practically all of the scenarios used in the book are based on actual situations I have encountered while working in different client organizations during the past twenty years. Sometimes I have revealed the organization's identity (with its permission), but most of the time I have had to use a fictitious name. There are still very strong taboos against admitting that your organization, department, or team is negative.

The book has two sections, each attacking negativity on a different front:

- Managing Individual and Team Negativity
- Managing Organizational Negativity

In Chapter 1 we look at the roots of negativity, why dealing with negativity is important, and the difference between temporary and pervasive negativity. In Chapter 2 we visit the cast of negativists, or the fourteen types of negative people. Both general and specific coping strategies for dealing with each of these types are delineated. You may even recognize some of the people who are driving you crazy at work.

Chapter 3 discusses the thirty strategies for coping with temporary bouts of negativity, whether these bouts are yours or belong to your team members. Strategies include using the tape recorder, having a favorite phrase, setting a time limit, and the standing ovation. These methods are easy to use and get immediate results. You may also find several of them quite funny.

In Chapter 4 we focus on what to do with the pervasive type of negativity—negativity that is extremely destructive to the work environment. We recommend using the accountability model for addressing this constant type of negativity.

The second section, Chapters 5 through 9, focuses on the three major causes of and solutions to organizational negativity: change, imbalance of trust and enablement, and norms (expected and accepted behavior).

In Chapter 5 we see how to prevent negativity by using the VISAR, the five ingredients for successful change, and doing the benefits and resisting factors analysis. This chapter also discusses people's various reactions to change and the organization's responsibility in managing change.

In Chapter 6 we present the trust matrix, which depicts the relationship between enablement and trust. The matrix shows you how to develop positive peak performers and avoid the negativity of being "bunker entrenched," "flying blind," and being "caged eagles."

The four-step process of changing negative norms into positive ones is demonstrated in Chapter 7. A case study, that of Cerro Medical Center, is used to bring these steps to life.

Additional strategies for eliminating organizational negativity are reviewed in Chapter 8: developing a learning environment, fulfilling staff needs, encouraging creativity, and hiring a "jollyologist."

In Chapter 9 we focus strictly on you, the reader. Here you learn that you have to equip yourself with a positive attitude even in the most negative situations.

I wrote this book for two major reasons. First, I care deeply about my clients' work environments. While consulting with a wide variety of clients for many years, I have uncovered a major, largely unexamined barrier to superior employee performance: negativity. In many of my consulting assignments, I have worked with staff members who were unhappy at their companies. They felt neither valued nor respected by their peers, managers, or organizations. I wanted to provide them with the tools for fighting negativity.

The second reason was to show my negative friends, colleagues, and family members that there is an alternative. One does not have to behave in a pessimistic way. Being optimistic reaps much bigger benefits.

This book will teach you many things:

- The steps you can take to transform a negative workplace into an upbeat, positive one
- Methods to help you hold people accountable for their negative behaviors (so they are less likely to repeat them)
- The common sources of workplace negativity and how you can learn to manage them
- How to help a colleague who has come down with the negativity bug
- How negativity is expressed and whether you are guilty of spreading it
- How to build an organization, department, or team that has high levels of positive behaviors, thus averting an attack of negativity

Here's a suggestion: When reading the book, do not think that every strategy, process, intervention, tip, or technique will work equally well for you, your negativist, or your organization. Be selective. Use the ones that will work best for you!

ACKNOWLEDGMENTS

I am indebted to all of the individuals in many different organizations and in my public seminars who were willing to share their "negativity" stories and experiences with me. They built the foundation for this book.

I am also grateful to Jim Milton, who several years ago invited me to do my first writing on this topic. In addition, I would like to recognize the International Society of Corporate Presidents, who, on several occasions, had me present this topic to them. It helped me develop my strong beliefs on how to cure organizational negativity.

My editor, Adrienne Hickey, deserves a lot of recognition as well. Not only did she believe that this topic would be one that would attract a wide audience, but she was also very persistent in seeing that the book was written. And thank you Bryan Kinney and Linda Oku for letting me "see" that this stuff made sense.

Finally, to my friends and family who had to manage on their own while I was writing. A special acknowledgment goes to Kitty, Gersh, SJ, and Len, who were constant comforts during this entire process.

Section I

MANAGING INDIVIDUAL AND TEAM NEGATIVITY

Chapter 1

WHAT IS WORKPLACE NEGATIVITY, WHAT ARE ITS CAUSES, AND HOW DOES IT SHOW ITSELF?

WHAT IS WORKPLACE NEGATIVITY?

Who has not experienced spurts of negativity about changes occurring at work? Who has not become negative when a trusted friend or colleague was let go because of downsizing? Who has not become negative when not given the plum assignment or not placed on the new project team? And who has not been put off by the individual who complains about everything the company does?

Everyone has reason to become negative about his or her work or his or her organization from time to time. But when negativity becomes a routine posture for you, your coworkers, and the entire company, it can begin to eat away at performance.

If problems such as the following exist at your company, negativity may be taking a toll:

- Work is constantly criticized by others
- Job security is lacking
- Good work is seldom praised or recognized
- Individuals work in isolation from others
- Destructive conflicts exist between departments
- Supervision is poor
- Opportunities for advancement or growth are small
- Top management decisions are not trusted
- Stress levels are too high or too low
- Departments are constantly being reorganized
- Fear of change is high
- Job fits are poor
- Ample resources are lacking
- Working conditions are poor

Workplace negativity is a virus that spreads rapidly from one person to another. An individual either brings the virus to the workplace or catches it there from other individuals or from the organization itself. Sometimes someone has a double dose of the virus—he or she is negative to start out with and then gets another dose of it at work.

Negativity is contagious. It can spread in a matter of minutes, and before anyone realizes what has happened, the entire workplace can be affected. But chicken soup and antibiotics are no cure, because this is not a physical illness. It is an attitude virus that causes negativity in all it touches.

Negativity shows itself when certain thoughts, moods, behaviors, or actions of an individual are communicated in the workplace. When too many of these behaviors are noticed by the negative individual's colleagues, or when their frequency is excessive, they can easily spread.

THE IMPACT OF WORKPLACE NEGATIVITY

U.S. companies lose about $3 billion a year to the effects of negativity, according to the Bureau of Labor Statistics. When negativity affects productivity or profitability, your company has a serious problem.

Whether the cause of the negativity is internal (the personality and communication style of the individual), external (inherent in the organizational culture), or a combination of the two, the results can be devastating. The effects of negativity are measurable and can lead to these outcomes:

- Increased customer complaints
- Increased error rates and a lessening of work quality
- Increased turnover
- Increased absences and lateness
- Increased personality conflicts
- Loss of morale and motivation
- Loss of loyalty to the organization
- Loss of creativity and innovation
- Loss of a competitive spirit

Let's look at each effect in depth.

INCREASED CUSTOMER COMPLAINTS

Cheryl, a customer service representative at a large Mercedes dealership ($60 million in sales last year) in Palm Beach, Florida, tends to see the downside of things. Often her negative take on life influences her work performance. When the dealership's clients call to complain about something minor that is wrong with their car, Cheryl becomes negative. She is condescending and sometimes rude. She cannot believe that customers get so upset about something wrong with their $80,000 cars while she makes half of that amount in a year's time. Customers do not like Cheryl's behavior. They complain to management about Cheryl's attitude and threaten to take their business elsewhere. Some have.

INCREASED ERROR RATES AND A LESSENING OF WORK QUALITY

Condo Property Management is quite a stressful place to work. It manages more than forty large apartment complexes in New York City. Pressure is intense, and the staff receives little support from management. Work hours are unpredictable and often exceed ten to twelve hours per day. Morale is low, and the staff has a negative attitude. In this negative environment, work quality declines and error rates increase.

INCREASED TURNOVER

Systems Right is one of the many new Internet start-ups in the Silicon Valley. More than 50 percent of its highly-sought-after engineers left during their first year at the company. During exit interviews, the engineers complained that they never had a voice in important decisions that affected their work. They felt a loss of self-esteem and quickly became negative about their work environment. Additionally, the engineers believed that they were over-supervised and soon lost respect for their senior managers.

INCREASED ABSENCES AND LATENESS

Elite Industries has an absence and lateness problem. A few of the seventy-five employees are very negative individuals and have begun to spread their negativity virus to other staff. As a result, many employees find the work environment unpleasant and try to avoid it as much as possible. They arrive late, leave early, or call in sick. This forces Elite Industries to pay excessive overtime and to hire temporary employees.

INCREASED PERSONALITY CONFLICTS

Anderson Paper Supplies is the major employer in the Northwest town in which it is located. Business has not been good, and the past several years have seen some staff cuts. Interpersonal conflicts have developed among staff because the company has let go some high performers and continues to keep some of the poorer performers. Everyone now seems to be critiquing his or her coworkers' value to the company.

LOSS OF MORALE AND MOTIVATION

Ken Clarkson is a manager in the marketing department at a beverage retailer in the Atlanta area. He is often very critical of his staff. He puts down their efforts, always finds fault with their performance, rarely tries to assist them, and is very moody. Ken has caused a lot of negativity in the department. Morale is so low that the staff will perform only when threatened.

LOSS OF LOYALTY TO THE ORGANIZATION

Profits at Barrington Industries, a computer chip manufacturer, are soaring. Barrington recently entered the Asian and African markets, and profits are up by more than 200 percent. A lot of good this has done the employees. While the salary and compensation packages of the CEO and other top management have quadrupled, the rest of the staff has received only modest gains. Employees wonder why they have been working so hard. They are losing or have lost their loyalty to Barrington. In addition, whenever an executive or even a managerial job becomes available, it is filled by an outsider even though there are qualified in-house candidates. Both of these corporate practices have led to high levels of negativity and diminishing levels of staff loyalty.

LOSS OF CREATIVITY AND INNOVATION

Mike is an instructional technologist hired by a large educational testing organization based in the West. He takes his job very seriously and considers his greatest strength to be his creativity and innovation. Mike's teammates, however, are very happy with the way things are and see no reason to change the current system of college entrance testing. They oppose Mike's ideas and insist that he be a team player. Mike goes along with the team's decisions even though he knows changes need to be made to the way students are tested for their entrance exams. After a time of always hearing no to his suggestions, he has stopped thinking creatively, has become bored, and feels negativity toward his teammates and the organization.

LOSS OF A COMPETITIVE SPIRIT

Organizational pride at Kings, a chain of discount stores in Southern California, is low. About half of the staff consists of struggling actors who obviously would rather not be at Kings. They berate their jobs and only talk about how soon they will quit. Their negative attitude toward their jobs is apparent to the rest of the staff (and to some of the customers as well). In fact, the rest of the staff has caught this negativity bug. When the organizational leaders try to build up a competitive spirit and to excite the staff about their respective stores, they cannot understand why there is little interest.

Each of these nine results of negativity affects the bottom line of an organization—its productivity and profitability. Negativity is a business issue and needs to be addressed as such.

NEGATIVITY AND THE THREE C'S: THE INFLUENCING FACTORS

Most of the cases of individual (and often companywide) negativity that I have witnessed over the years seem traceable to one or more of these factors:

1. Lack or loss of competence
2. Lack or loss of community
3. Lack or loss of control

LACK OR LOSS OF COMPETENCE

Every day at work, at an ever-increasing rate, we are faced with challenges to our competence. We are constantly asking ourselves if our abilities are sufficient to meet the needs of the rapidly changing work environment. You may be asking yourself these or similar questions right now: Will I be able to operate that new spreadsheet? Can I figure out how to do that video conferencing? Will I be able to work on a virtual team, manage telecommuters, use the new computer system, and learn the nuances of the new product that I have to sell within twenty-four hours? Will I be able to program the robotic or do the PowerPoint presentation?

If we believe we cannot do these things effectively or as well as others, our confidence level decreases. When confidence level decreases, self-esteem decreases. When self-esteem decreases, we fear the test of learning any new competency. This cycle increases the likelihood that we will become negative.

Case Study

As a result of a major reorganization, a manager at a Southern California utility company was recently transferred to the newly created Business Development Department. The skills needed in this high-profile department are very different from those that the manager previously needed. Now she must supervise the fourteen-person staff who sell and market the company's services. Previously she was in an operational position and was responsible for getting out the CEO's monthly status report. To make matters worse, she is faced with a rapid learning curve. She has to know this new information as of yesterday. Plus, she has never supervised a staff larger than two.

As a result of this change, the manager has become quite negative. She questions whether she will be able to quickly develop these new competencies.

LACK OR LOSS OF COMMUNITY

Think about the people with whom you are currently working. Think about those with whom you worked two years, one year, or six months ago. Through reorganizations, downsizing, mergers, and so forth we lose the people we get accustomed to working with, the people who get to know us. This loss of familiarity is often a leading cause of negativity. Then there are the individuals who work remotely or virtually, who are constantly traveling or telecommuting. They also experience the loss of the work community and a sense of belonging to something. These situations, as well, increase negativity.

Case Study

Rob, a senior engineer at a major software development company in the South, was assigned a few months ago to a new innovative project, which, at the time, he was very excited to be part of. The project, to make all training programs Web-based, would take about one year to complete. Rob is a fun-loving, extroverted guy and has been with the company for three years. Six months into the project, Rob is miserable. Even though he finds the work fascinating, he feels he is working in isolation with limited human interactions. He is part of a virtual team. He never gets to see anyone on the team, as its members are scattered all over the world. They have weekly conference calls, and the majority of communication is done via e-mail. Rob misses the camaraderie of his collocated teams and is quite negative about his current work situation. He is wondering if he will last another half-year on this assignment.

LACK OR LOSS OF CONTROL

The third C that often leads to negativity, lack or loss of control, is the feeling of powerlessness or a lack of being part of the decision-making that affects one's work. A person in this state of mind tends to question the importance of his or her work contribution and the organization for which he or she is working. Losses of commitment or loyalty are usually secondary factors associated with lack or loss of control.

Case Study

Andy has been a supervisor at a London electronics manufacturing company for the past twelve years. He was hired right after graduation and worked his way up through the ranks. Strong leadership and a strict sense of control over staff, especially the hourly worker, have always been the norm for the company's supervisors and managers. Andy has been rewarded for his leadership style and was next in line to become the department manager. That is, until recently. About seven months ago the CEO had a major change in philosophy on how the organization should be structured. He became an avid believer in getting the work done in teams. He has spent the past four months radically transforming the organization into a team-based one, greatly altering how decision-making takes place. Now "the staff" (formerly known as "the workers") makes most of the decisions on how the work gets done. Supervisors and managers act more as facilitators, helping out when needed by providing resources or doing strategic planning. Andy is not happy with this change. He liked being in control and seeing the immediate impact of his words and actions. He cannot adjust to this new style of management and is questioning his future with the company.

THE THREE C'S AND CHANGE

There is a common theme running through the Three C's—change. Continual change is the norm is the workplace now. It is no longer good enough for organizations to get individuals to accept change; they have to get people to embrace change enthusiastically in order to remain competitive in today's fast-paced world. Many senior managers have asked me why workplace negativity is on the rise in this time of economic prosperity. The answer is not all that complex. Constant change at work makes us question our competence, our community (Who are these people I work with? What do I know about them? Can I trust them? What do they know about me?), and our control over our own work.

Figure 1-1: Perception and Negativity

Our perceptions are influenced by our experiences, our values, the views and opinions of the significant people in our lives, and our self-esteem and self-confidence. Individuals may have very different reactions to the same situation or stimulus. A few examples illustrate this point.

Situation

You get an e-mail that the boss, the president, or the CEO needs to see you ASAP (there are no other specifics).

Response

People who are negative or who have a negative perception will dread this news. They may think that the boss wants to yell at them, give them a more difficult assignment, or fire them. People with a positive attitude or perception see the situation as an opportunity. They may think that they are getting some positive praise for a job well done, being put on a special project, or getting a promotion.

Situation

You've had a really bad day at work.

Response

Negative people let this affect their life outside of work. They go home and complain, get stressed or distressed. They blame themselves or others. They don't drop it; they keep thinking or talking about it. People with a positive perception are able to separate this bad day from the rest of their life; they do not let it get to them as much and forget about it much faster.

Situation

When you arrive at the airport for a business trip you hear that your flight has been delayed for two hours owing to mechanical difficulties.

Response

Negative people gripe, yell, sulk, or withdraw from the situation. Positive people accept the situation; they may read, work on the laptop, make phone calls, take a nap, and so on.

NEGATIVITY AND PHYSIOLOGY

Negativity is directly linked to physiology. The amygdala, part of the brain's cortex (the reasoning and rational part of the brain), developed during the stone age. The amygdala equipped us with the fight-or-flight response. This was a very important role for the early brain: a warning device that protected us from danger. Encountering a mammoth or a saber-toothed tiger, one could have chosen to fight it or to flee quickly. The amygdala is still part of the brain, but we have much fewer opportunities to use it. When we are put into a situation where our reaction is to flee or to fight, we often cannot. For example, an employee who you feel has been put on Earth to make your life miserable is acting up, and you would like to really get him (fight) or totally avoid him (flight). Of course, this would not be appropriate managerial behavior. When they feel trapped, angry, distressed, or helpless in situations and cannot flee or fight, many people become negative. That becomes their conditioned response.

HEREDITY VERSUS ENVIRONMENT

When talking about what makes someone appear to be a negative person, we must briefly mention the old controversy of heredity versus environment. You were probably taught in high school biology that most scientists believe people to be a combination of both, and our moods, behaviors, actions, and personality reflect that mixture. This combination of heredity and environment as influencing factors in how we behave is still believed to be true by most behavioral scientists. Pertaining to the heredity link, recent scientific research has identified a gene that is now known as the "mood" gene. In fact, prenatal research being conducted at Georgetown University's Department of Physiology for the past several years has found that even within the womb personality or mood differences can be detected.

HOW WE COMMUNICATE NEGATIVITY

Negativity, just like positivism, is an attitude we communicate at work in three major ways:

1. Through our words or verbally
2. Through our body language or nonverbally
3. Through vocal sounds or paralanguage.

Verbal Communication

Negativity is expressed through the words we use. Statements such as the following communicate negativity and encourage others to become negative as well:

- "It will never work."
- "Where did we ever get that new CEO from? She does not seem to know what she is doing."
- "No, never, impossible, not a chance."
- "He's always doing that. It's his fault!"
- "Bad idea, sounds stupid, no way."

Nonverbal Communication

In addition to our verbal behaviors, we express our feelings and thoughts (our attitudes) nonverbally. Facial expressions such as a smile or a frown; eye contact or the lack thereof; body gestures such as crossed arms; and how we sit, stand, move, and walk into a meeting, or even walk through the corridors, are all considered nonverbal behaviors.

Nonverbal gestures are powerful messages that influence how we react to others. Years ago I had a boss, Jim, who was very inconsistent in his attitude. Some days he would be incredibly negative, whereas on other days he was quite the optimist. This was hard on the staff. We never knew what to expect. So to prepare us for the kind of day we were going to have with Jim, each morning we would gather around a window that looked out onto the parking lot and watch the way Jim got out of his car. Based on his body language, we would be ready for the day. If he slammed the door and walked with his head down or had clenched fists, we knew we were in for a bad day. We kept clear of him. On the other hand, a smiling face, erect posture, a lilt in his walk, or a quiet closing of the car door assured us that this would be a great day. Those were the days we would approach him and get whatever we wanted.

When you think about it, we are constantly communicating at work, even though we may never utter a word. If there is another human being around, we are communicating.

People are making judgments based on what they see, and most people believe their own judgments to be true. A bit of advice: Try to be aware of how you are coming across with your body language. You might be sending out messages you had not intended. Most interpersonal communication experts believe that our nonverbal communication has the greatest influence on how others perceive us at work. They estimate that about 50 percent of our message to others in a face-to-face situation is interpreted based on how we look, 25 percent on what we say, and the final 25 percent on paralanguage.

Paralanguage (Vocals)

The third factor that influences how others view us at work in terms of our attitude is called paralanguage. This is how we speak our words. Examples of paralanguage include volume—(how loudly or softly we speak), frequency (how often we speak), pronunciation, accent, emphasis, and voice tone. For example, the person who whines (and never brings cheese) is often viewed as a complainer with a negative attitude; or the person who speaks very loudly comes across as aggressive and wanting his or her own way.

NEGATIVITY IS A HABIT

A habit is defined as something we do automatically, without thinking about it. Negativity is a habit. Being positive is also a habit. Negativity can be someone's normal reaction to life, or it could come up when one is stressed, anxious, depressed, annoyed, angry, or disappointed.

One of the best ways to reduce negativity at work is to have people turn their negative habits into more positive ones. It always amazes me that most people who come across as negative are not aware of their behavior. From my experience, I would estimate that the percentage is about 80. There are three reasons why most negative people are unaware that others perceive them as such:

1. Negative people believe there is nothing wrong with their behavior. They have always behaved this way, and they never think about their attitude.

2. Negative people see others as negative and think that if others are negative it is OK for them to be negative as well. Or, in some organizations, negativity becomes the norm, and one learns to behave like others.

3. Most negative people do not get feedback on their negativity. Team members may feel that it is up to their leader to give feedback to the negativist. Customers may not say anything but just stay away the

next time. Employees are probably afraid to confront their negative bosses.

Most individuals in the workplace believe that negativity is part of someone's personality. They feel that they just have to learn how to live with different personalities because they cannot change someone's personality. This belief is both correct and incorrect.

We have to recognize that different people have different personality types, and that it is very difficult to change personality. Most psychologists would say that personality is formed by the time we are five. Nevertheless, we have to look at the workplace behaviors that are causing someone to come across as negative and try to change them. We never want to focus on changing personality, only on changing behaviors. Whereas changing someone's personality is extremely difficult, if not impossible, changing behaviors is challenging, but it can be done.

In short, we have to get people to recognize their negative habits and then identify positive behaviors to replace them. By focusing on behaviors (and performance), not personality, negativity can be changed. If a team member does not recognize his or her negative habit, we need to give that person feedback on it. This way the teammate can work on changing his or her habits. If this strategy does not work, we will have to become more serious and confront the negativity (discussed in Chapter 4).

It is also up to us to ask others about our attitude at work. We should constantly try to get feedback on how we are communicating our thoughts, actions, and feelings.

SUMMARY

In this chapter we defined what a negative attitude is, what causes individuals to become negative, and how negativity is expressed—verbally, nonverbally, and through paralanguage. We also saw that negativity is a habit, one that many individuals do not even know that they have. In Chapter 2 we look at fourteen different types of negativists and the strategies for managing their negativity.

Chapter 2

THE CAST OF NEGATIVISTS

As discussed in Chapter 1, people demonstrate their negative attitudes in many different ways. In this chapter we present general strategies for working with negative individuals, describe fourteen types of negative individuals (negativists), and give you a specific strategy for handling each one.

GENERAL COPING STRATEGIES FOR WORKING WITH NEGATIVISTS

▪ Recognize that an attitude problem exists.

The first step is to recognize that someone is expressing negativity in the workplace. Do not ignore it if it is affecting that person's performance, your performance, the performance of others, or relationships with your clients or customers.

▪ Acknowledge any underlying causes for the negative attitude.

As we know, negativity has many causes. The factors could include personal problems, work-related stress, a difficult boss, job insecurity, loss of loyalty, lack of growth or advancement opportunities, and so forth. It helps to get the person to see the causes for his or her negativity. It is also important to recognize that what is causing the negativity is often justified and that the negativist has the right to feel that way.

- Help the person take responsibility.

It is ultimately the responsibility of the negative person to change his or her negative attitude and behaviors at work. Even though the person may have every right to feel the way he or she does, it is still not appropriate for the workplace. As a team member or boss, you need to help your colleague recognize this and to have him or her take ownership.

- Replace negative, inappropriate reactions with different, more acceptable ones.

Even though we just said that it is the job of the negativist to change his or her actions, you may need to help. The person may not know what to do differently to come across as more positive. It will often be up to you to specify exactly what that is.

- Instill positive attitudes in others.

Be the role model for your negativists through your actions and behaviors. You can prevent their negativity by instilling in them the positivist bug. If you do that, they may never catch the negativity virus again.

THE CAST OF NEGATIVISTS

1. The Locomotives
2. The Perfectionists

1. THE LOCOMOTIVES

The locomotives express their negativity by steam-rolling over people. They are very angry and hostile and take out their frustrations on others. They come across as being tyrannical, autocratic, and dictatorial. Their favorite saying is "My way or the highway." Here's an example:

Locomotive: *(standing over a staff member with one hand in a fist and finger pointing with the other)* Do it now. No discussion. It better happen by two o'clock! *(walking away)*

Soon-to-Be Negativist: But, . . .

Locomotive: No buts here. Just get to it.

Soon-to-Be Negativist: *(mouth is wide open in disbelief)*

The Solution

Do not take it! Describe how the person's behavior affects your work, express how it makes you feel, and specify how you need to be communicated to differently. Be assertive with the locomotives.

2. THE PERFECTIONISTS

If something is not perfect, the perfectionist becomes negative. This person's standards of performance are not realistic, and even excellent work that is praised by others is unacceptable to him or her. An example of this is the perfectionist parent whose child graduates valedictorian from high school with a 98.5 grade-point average. The parent asks the child (seriously) what happened to the other 1.5 points. We see perfectionist behavior at work all the time. Some managers have excellent performers but never rate them in the top category on performance reviews. The favorite saying of the perfectionist is "It could have been better."

Let's listen in to a meeting that the perfectionist bank branch supervisor is holding with the tellers:

Perfectionist Supervisor: It's now taking us an average of fifty seconds to serve each customer who comes to one of our windows. I want to bring that time down.

Brave Teller: The average time at the other branches is seventy seconds. We're doing extremely well. The national average is seventy-five.

Perfectionist Supervisor: I'll never be satisfied with our service time, unless it gets down to zero.

The Solution

Do not take these people's statements seriously. They are expressing their own inadequacies, not yours. Try to work with them so that they can set realistic expectations for themselves and others.

3. THE ICE PEOPLE/RESISTERS

Any change, no matter how small, can upset the ice people and cause an outbreak of negativity. They love the status quo. Try to change it and their resistance will flare up.

Early on in their lives, they got the message that change was a negative, and they find every reason to fight it. The ice people usually do not openly express their opposition to change. They do it more subtly. They may even say that the change is good and that they support it, but then just won't implement it. The extreme ice people may even resort to sabotage if they find a particular change exceptionally threatening. Their favorite saying is "I liked it better the old way."

Here are two ice people talking to each other about an impending system change:

Ice Person No. 1: I can't believe they are bringing in that new system. It'll mean a lot more work for all of us. The clients will benefit but not we analysts.

Ice Person No. 2: I thought I heard you tell that IS guy that you thought the new system was a great idea.

Ice Person No. 1: Of course I did. They can't think that any of us oppose it. But you can be sure I'll do anything not to make it work.

Ice Person No. 2: That's the spirit! All they ever want to do around here is bring in change. Don't they realize that people don't like change and would rather keep things the way they are?

Ice Person No. 1: They'll never learn, I guess.

The Solution

The best strategy is to try to involve these people in the change. If they are part of the process or come up with the change themselves, their resistance will decrease tremendously. You may also want to gradually introduce the change to them so that they have time to get used to it. Sudden change is an open introduction to their heightened negativity.

4. THE NOT-MY-JOB–ERS

These individuals express their negativity by refusing to do any task, no matter how simple, if they decide it is not part of their job responsibilities. It is often their way of getting back at their colleagues, their managers, or the organization itself because of their unhappiness with how they are being treated. Their favorite saying is "It is not part of my job description to do that." Here's an example:

Overworked Colleague: Andy, could you drop this package off for me?

Not-My-Job–er: That's not my job.

Overworked Colleague: I'll drop off the package if you answer my calls.

Not-My-Job–er: Well, that's not what I'm supposed to do either!

Overworked Colleague: Andy, just what exactly is your job description?

Not-My-Job–er: I was hired to take inventory, check shipment dates, do status reports, and trace lost packages.

(Discouraged by this unhelpful attitude, the beleaguered colleague goes off to deliver the package herself.)

The Solution

Try to find training and development opportunities for the Not-My-Job–ers. They are seeking growth and advancement. When they feel they are on a dead-end career road, they lose their enthusiasm for work and try to do as little as possible.

5. The Rumormongers

Rumormongers take out their negativity toward work by spreading rumors. They feel a sense of importance when the stories they created begin to circulate or when others have strong reactions to what they are saying. Rumormongers also sense a loss of control over their environments or other people. Rumors help them regain that control. Their favorite saying is "Let me tell you what is really happening."

Rumormongers especially like to spread rumors about

- senior managers
- reorganizations or job cuts
- other people's salaries
- the fast-trackers
- what competing companies offer their employees
- who is dating whom at the company

They perceive these topics to be their most powerful weapons in gaining control over others, even if it is only temporary control.

The Solution

The best solution is to give people in the organization the information and facts they need. When you do this, there is little motivation for them to listen to the rumor-mongers.

6. THE PESSIMISTS

Pessimists experience the world as an unpleasant place. They expect the world to fall down on them, and if it doesn't, they do everything possible to help bring it down. They are unhappy with the way things are, and no matter what you try to do for them, it does not appear to make a difference. They are often the same outside of work as well. Their favorite saying is "The tunnel will never end." Here's an example:

Neighbor: Congratulations! I hear your daughter is getting married.

Pessimist: Right. It's another big expense for me.

Neighbor: But it's such a happy occasion.

Pessimist: Yeah, for everyone else except me. I have to pay the bill.

Neighbor: Have a small wedding then. Your daughter is great. She'll understand.

Pessimist: Then everyone will dislike me and call me cheap. You can never win. Things are always working against me. *(Try to hear the paralanguage also.)*

Neighbor: Nice talking to you!

The Solution

You probably won't be able to change pessimists' attitude easily, so, for a start, focus on having them adopt some new specific positive habits to take the place of their existing negative ones. With practice and reinforcement, these new behaviors will gradually begin to replace the old ones.

7. THE UNCOMMITTEDS

These are the people who do not take their jobs seriously, making their teammates' work more difficult. Work is a very low priority for them. Their focus at work is trying to do as little as possible so as to find time to take care of personal matters or other interests. They sense no urgency in getting the work done. Their favorite saying is "It can wait." Here's an example:

Teammate: Jennifer, did you get the team report up to Mr. Davis in time?

Jennifer: Oh, let me see. No, I didn't. I have it right here.

Teammate: The team had all agreed that we would meet the deadline.

Jennifer: I didn't think it was that important. I had other things to do.

Teammate: It was very important.

Jennifer: Whatever! *(With the annoying-sounding paralanguage.)*

The Solution

Uncommitteds need to have clear goals, standards, and expectations established and then communicated to them. They also need close monitoring to see how they are performing.

8. THE CRITICIZERS

Have a creative approach? Do you have a different way of doing something or a new suggestion? If you do, the criticizers will knock it down. Their mission is to disagree with anything that is said. They like to be right, no matter what. They find problems wherever they go, never opportunities. Criticizers will never give positive feedback but will always jump on you for a mistake. Their favorite saying is "Bad idea."

Here are two work colleagues discussing an upcoming business trip:

Colleague: Let's drive instead of flying. We'll get there faster.

Criticizer: What, are you crazy?

Colleague: Why do you say that?

Criticizer: It's just a bad idea.

Colleague: OK. Let's fly up tonight so we can be fresh for tomorrow afternoon's presentation.

Criticizer: Where are you coming from? Bad idea.

Colleague: Why?

Criticizer: Trust me on it. You have less experience. Your thinking is illogical.

Colleague: Please be specific and explain yourself.

Criticizer: What, now you can't understand me? What's wrong with you?

The Solution

Criticizers like to give negative feedback, but they rarely are specific. Ask them for examples, evidence, or their reasoning for disagreeing. You must be persistent and not give up. They will find it hard to come up with examples or to explain their criticisms. When you ask for details about what they are saying they will often back down with their unproductive criticism.

9. THE CRYBABIES

Crybabies behave like children who don't get their way. Not getting their way causes their negativity. They frown, withdraw, go off on a tirade, and literally cry.

I once worked with a very bright and extremely well known organizational development consultant who was highly regarded by all of his clients. Oftentimes, however, when projects were running into roadblocks or the clients weren't giving him everything he asked for, he would go into his office, lock it, and pout and whine. The clients would come by and apologize and say sweet and nice things to him. Then he would return to work.

The favorite saying of the crybaby is "Nobody loves me." A crybaby contractor, for instance, would complain something like this: "The pressure is getting to be too much. I'm not getting your full cooperation. I'm getting all stressed out. I want to do a great job for you. It's really hard doing this work."

The Solution

These people need a supportive environment and constant encouragement that they are doing well. You also have to lower their stress and pressure levels.

10. THE SACRIFICERS

Sacrificers are the bleeding hearts of the office. They come in early and stay late. They'll do anything you ask them to. But they will, in a self-deprecating way, complain about their workload, difficult employees, and customers or bosses. They often have unpleasant personal lives and sublimate their unhappiness by trying to make work be the answer. What brings out their negativity is the feeling that their great efforts are going unappreciated. When this occurs, their favorite saying is "I have given up my life for this company and nobody cares." Here's an example:

Sacrificer: I'll do it. Don't worry about me. Go home.

Appreciative Team Member: I can't do that to you. I'll stay.

Sacrificer: I really don't have anything to do so I might as well stay and finish the report.

Appreciative Staff Member: Thanks. I'll see you in the morning. Goodnight.

Sacrificer (to himself): Right. I'll just slave away. No one really gives a darn.

Appreciative Team Member: Are you sure? I hope I'm not putting you out.

Sacrificer: What are another few hours. I've already been here for ten.

The Solution

You must give these people constant positive feedback on how much you appreciate their contributions and hard work. They especially like recognition in front of their colleagues and teammates. If you really want them to remain positive, periodically send them e-mail in which you praise their commitment (and be sure to cc the boss).

11. THE SELF-CASTIGATORS

These people get upset with themselves and then become negative. They find fault with their work performance, appearance, career progress, socioeconomic status, educational background, and so on. They have a very low self-concept and will often say to themselves, "You idiot! Why did you do that?" or "What's wrong with you? You should have known better." Quite often it is their perception about themselves that is the problem. On paper, they are doing pretty well, but they never see it that way. Their favorite saying to others is "I'll take the blame, and I could have done better." Here's an example:

Supervisor: You know, Elliot, this wasn't your best work.

Self-Castigator: You're right. I can never do anything right. I hope you don't fire me for this.

Supervisor: Elliot, I have no intention of firing you. You usually do excellent work around here.

Self-Castigator: You're just saying that. I know the truth. I'm really not that good. I'll try harder though.

Supervisor: Whatever you say, Elliot.

The Solution

Find any strategy to build up these people's self-esteem. They are in desperate need of some ego boosts. You could also gather evidence to prove that they are wrong about themselves and then present them with that evidence.

I once worked with a quality assurance director who believed that he and his department were causing the downfall of the organization. I had to give him documentation that the mistakes and problems were not coming from his area. In fact, his department was one of the few that had kept the company afloat for the previous few years. It was only when I showed him this evidence that his self-castigation disappeared.

12. THE SCAPEGOATERS

Because they cannot accept the responsibility or take the blame for their own mistakes, scapegoaters shift the onus to others, especially when they are in their negative moods. They seem to feel better seeing others squirm or get into trouble. Their favorite saying is "I didn't do it, it was _____." Here's an example:

Marketing Department Manager: Josh, I need those sales figures to complete my new product analysis.

Scapegoater: You never told me about this before.

Marketing Department Manager: Check out the e-mail I sent you last Friday.

Scapegoater: I never got it. Blame our Intranet system, not me.

Marketing Department Manager: The system shows that you received and saved the e-mail.

Scapegoater: Oh, those figures. I told Bryan to do them. You mean he hasn't got them to you yet? What's wrong with that guy?

Marketing Department Manager: Hasn't Bryan been overseas working on the Beta account for the past month?

Scapegoat: Well, . . . *(To himself: "Who can I blame now?")*

The Solution

Scapegoaters stop this behavior when you give them very specific examples of how their errors, mistakes, or miscalculations were the problem. You cannot be vague with them. They find it difficult to shift the blame when you are specific.

13. THE EGGSHELLS

The eggshells are very sensitive people, and the slightest thing said to them, if misconstrued, causes them to crack. When they get too many cracks they become negative. Their favorite saying is "Don't let me know, I can't deal with it."

Denise, an IT manager at a rapidly growing Silicon Valley company, always took very innocent comments the wrong way. If a colleague said to her on her way out of the door, "What, only twelve hours today?" Denise would feel she was not working hard enough. Then she would jump to the conclusion that the colleague believed she was shirking her responsibilities. Eventually she would crack and start leaking negativity wherever she went. She'd say things like "How dare I get criticized! I work hard around here" or "This company doesn't deserve me if they think I'm not pulling my weight."

The Solution

When you have to give these people some critical or constructive feedback, make sure it is *not* brief and directly to the point (as it usually should be with others). Get into it slowly, never making it personal, and be sure the person has understood your point before you move on. Doing this will minimize the big cracks from occurring.

14. The Micros

Remember when you were in high school and you wrote what you believed to be a great paper, original story, or composition? Did the teacher ever focus on the smallest details or mistakes and forget about the big picture? Did she focus on a couple of grammatical errors or a misspelled word or that you didn't cross your t's? That teacher was being micro. A micro's favorite saying is "I need to check that again; I must have missed something."

We see many micros at the office, too:

- The sales presentation went splendidly, but the micro focused on the one bit of unimportant information you left out.
- You just finished facilitating a training session to overwhelming rave reviews. Twenty-four out of twenty-five participants rate the program as excellent. One gives it a fair. Your training director focuses only on the one fair and never mentions that all the other reviews were excellent.
- During a creative brainstorming, the micro questions the rationale behind each idea. He becomes very uncomfortable without all the information and details.

Micros like to focus on the smallest details. When they do that a lot, or inappropriately, they come across as being too picky, too negative.

The Solution

Have these people get into the habit of evaluating the entire project or assignment. They are great discerners of information. What they need, however, is to be more macro, to see the larger context. Ask them for the main point of something, the overall goal, the major problems, the biggest benefit, the greatest strength or weakness, the main objectives, the overall direction of the project, and so forth. This tactic gets the micro to think in a more broad-based fashion. When they focus on the big picture, they no longer seem negative.

Now that we have identified the cast of negativists and both general and specific strategies for working with each of them, let's return to an earlier discussion on how to transform their negative habits into positive ones.

TURNING NEGATIVE HABITS INTO POSITIVE ONES

We have just described fourteen types of people who display their negativity in slightly different ways. Their behaviors do not sound all that bad, especially when we jest about them. But we need to take these negative behaviors in earnest because they do affect other people and the work environment. We need to take action to help these individuals to communicate their attitudes in a more positive way.

Some negative habits are relatively easy to change; others can be more difficult. The difficulty arises because the habits are interconnected. A single negative behavior can become a cue for another negative behavior, which in turn may be a cue for still another. In this way, one develops habit sequences that form strong patterned behaviors.

How long does it take to turn a negative work-related habit into a more positive one? Many of the relatively easy work-related habits could be changed within a week. The more difficult ones will take at least three weeks. That is, if the negativist practices the new positive behavior consistently for at least three weeks, it will become the predominant response pattern. In this manner, the old negative habit gets replaced with the new positive one.

When an individual recognizes his or her negative habit or is given feedback on a negative habit, this person can use either, or both, of these following methods for change.

TWENTY-ONE CONSECUTIVE DAYS

This method consists of five easy steps that negativists can follow on their own or with the help of a teammate or manager. As we already know, some individuals will be able to recognize their work-related negative behaviors and be able to follow these steps on their own. *Others will have to be told of their negative behaviors and helped closely through this process.* In the following examples, individuals have become aware of their negative habits and want to turn them into positive ones.

1. Describe the current negative habit in specific terms.

To identify the specific behaviors you need to change, you have to identify what they are and the situations in which they occur. The more you know this, the easier it will be to change.

Here are some examples:

- "When I am at staff meetings, my natural reaction is to disagree with the boss before hearing her out."
- "At client meetings, I try to get my point across first and pretend I am listening to their reply."
- "When that difficult staff member asks me a question, I answer in a terse, sarcastic way."

2. Describe the impact the negative behavior is having.

The impact on relationships, performance, sales, customer service, and so on is the main reason for changing a negative behavior. If there is no impact, it is not a problem that needs to be immediately addressed (or addressed at all). Nevertheless, you may want to figure out, for your own personal development, why you do it or what situations bring out this negativity.

Here are some examples:

- "I am viewed as someone who is always challenging the boss's authority and not supporting the company."
- "The client does not feel as if I have their best interest at heart and may find another vendor."
- "Staff members will stop coming to me when true problems arise, and I may be left in the dark."

3. Describe the new, more positive behavior to use.

You will need to develop an action plan for how you will implement this new habit or positive behavior. You may also want to practice it or script it out before trying it. The latter technique builds self-confidence.

Here are some examples:

- "Let the boss finish, describe my position, but still support the organizational direction."
- "Maintain eye contact with the customer and show concern for his point of view."
- "Remain calm, professional, and receptive to staff members when expressing myself."

4. Be consistent and persistent.

Part-time application does not develop new habits. Consistency and persistency are the only way to develop new habits. It takes at least twenty-one consecutive days to break an ingrained negative habit or to add a new, positive one to your repertoire. (The number twenty-one comes from the work of the well-known behavior modification practitioners Skinner, Thorndike, and Watson.) Just because you were able to do it for a day or a few days will not guarantee that it has become the new way.

5. Get feedback from those whom you could trust to be honest on how your new habit is developing.

Have others witnessed a change? Are you coming across in a more positive way? Think carefully about who might be able to help you and give you feedback on how you are doing. Building strong support around you facilitates the mastering of positive habits.

REPOH

REPOH is the second model that can be used to change behaviors. It is a sports training model that leading coaches and athletes have been using for many years. While attending an organizational development convention several years ago, I heard Pat Summitt of the University of Tennessee speak on REPOH. Summitt has one of the best records of any basketball coach, male or female, in Division 1 schools. She attributes the success of many of her players to the REPOH method. I have only recently started using the model with clients who need coaching on their negativity. It has been quite successful.

Teach your negativists this acronym. They will love it. It will enable them to replace their negative words, expressions, and gestures with much more positive ones.

Repeat
> The more you repeat the new identified behavior,

Easier
> the easier it becomes; then

Practice
> the more you will practice it and

Often
> the more often you will do it,

Habit
> eventually it becomes a habit.

Here's an example:

Repeat
> "Whenever I have a great opportunity to close a deal,

I'll think of all the reasons why it will succeed (instead of all the reasons why it will not)."

Easier

"The more I think only of the positive reasons, the easier it will become for me to do this."

Practice

"The more I think only of the positive reasons, the more I'll practice thinking of only the positive reasons."

Often

"The more I practice this new behavior and become successful with it (I get feedback on my own or from others that it is working), the more often I'll do it."

Habit

"Eventually, with consistency and persistency, this behavior of thinking of positive outcomes instead of negative ones will become my new positive habit."

SUMMARY

Both with the general coping strategies discussed at the beginning of this chapter and with the specific ones for each of the fourteen cast members, you should have a better handle on managing or working with your own negativists. Keep in mind that your goal here is to change these negative behaviors into positive ones. That is when twenty-one consecutive days and REPOH become valuable tools for you.

Chapter 3

THIRTY QUICK FIXES FOR OVERCOMING INDIVIDUAL AND TEAM NEGATIVITY

In this chapter you will find thirty techniques to abate negativity when it strikes an individual or a group of individuals at work. These techniques work best for occasional or temporary occurrences of negativity. More involved measures are required when the negativity is ongoing or severe (discussed in Chapter 4). Keep in mind that not all of these strategies will work for everyone. You have to find the ones that suit your sometimes-negative colleagues the best. These strategies can also work for the rare and through-no-fault-of-your-own times when you become negative.

The thirty strategies are:

1. Recognize the negativity trigger points.
2. Take a timeout.
3. Provide an attitude checkup.
4. Encourage laughter or joke logs.

5. Use the tape recorder.

6. Keep thoughts in the present.

7. Have a favorite saying.

8. Set a time limit for negativity.

9. Set ground rules.

10. See the bigger picture—the 2M approach.

11. Look at quality criticism as a plus.

12. Collect funny objects.

13. Reenergize with IQT.

14. Use flipside thinking.

15. Stop the thought!

16. Wear a rubber band and snap away the negativity.

17. Use 3, 2, 1 . . . 1, 2, 3.

18. Resolve conflicts—the win-win approach.

19. Surround yourself with optimistic people.

20. Be your own best friend.

21. Play your winners.

22. Provide a new opportunity or skill.

23. Do something to help others.

24. Take the AAA approach.

25. Reward yourself for being positive.

26. Lock in the negativity at work.

27. Assign numbers to certain words.

28. Use the standing ovation.

29. Take some pictures.

30. Buy some whips.

STRATEGY 1: RECOGNIZE THE NEGATIVITY TRIGGER POINTS

If you can help your team member recognize the trigger or catalyst for his or her negativity, the blow will be lessened. Additionally, once the cause is known, such as the over-demanding boss or the office whiner, the teammate may be able to learn to live with it and not allow himself or herself to become so negative. It is even possible that the negativist, with practice, will be able to perceive the stimulus triggering the negativity.

SCENARIO

Denise is a highly competent and usually motivated legal assistant who looks forward to her workdays. Nonetheless, at least one or two days a week her supervisor notices that Denise, especially in the mornings, is in a negative mood. She frowns a lot, speaks in a low and inaudible voice, and is overly critical of the clients and the partners.

Denise's supervisor pointed out these behaviors to Denise and tried to find out what was triggering them. After a couple of discussions, the trigger that sets off her negativity was identified. When Denise goes onto the highway and sees that the traffic is really bad on some mornings, she gets down on herself for not being able to afford to live closer to downtown. This sets her up for a negative start to the day at work. The supervisor explained to Denise that the trigger for her temporary negativity is the traffic and that she is fine until she encounters it.

Once Denise realizes what the trigger for her negativity is, she can do something to alter the trigger or her reaction. Perhaps leaving earlier, figuring out how she could move closer to work, getting books on tape for the drive, or saying to herself "Where else do cars go?" will enable Denise to manage her negativity and not let it affect her performance or the workplace.

STRATEGY 2: TAKE A TIMEOUT

Get your colleague who is in danger of having a temporary bout of negativity to take a timeout and remove him or her from the negative situation or environment. Five or ten minutes away can do wonders and keep that person in his or her positive mindset. He or she can take a walk outside, go to the cafeteria, or sit in an empty conference room. Many organizations now have rooms designated as quiet or relaxation rooms where staff can go for a few minutes to unwind or recharge. When the individuals return to their jobs, they are much more productive.

SCENARIO

Sharon Sager is a performer's representative at a talent agency in Nashville. She is constantly bombarded with phone and e-mail messages from clients who are unhappy with their representation. They complain about the dollar amounts of their contracts, the locations of their performances, the other entertainers on the bill with them, and so on. All of these complaints put Sharon in a negative mood. Whenever Sharon is experiencing one of these negativity episodes, she opens her desk drawer and takes out a sign that says "Negativity Break" in big, bold, multicolored letters. She flashes it around the office to all of her colleagues. Then she goes into one of the nearby client meeting rooms, grabs a cup of tea, and recharges her battery. About five to ten minutes later she is back at her desk in a much more positive frame of mind.

In many organizations or companies, staff cannot "remove" themselves from a negative situation. They will need to learn stress reduction techniques such as deep breathing or muscle relaxation.

STRATEGY 3: PROVIDE AN ATTITUDE CHECK-UP

At the same time that you give your team or staff their quarterly or semi-annual performance review, also give them some feedback on how they communicate their attitude at work. Let them know how they are coming across to others through their words, their behavior, and, as previously described, their paralanguage. Emphasize that their attitude often influences how successful they will be on the job. If attitude feedback is presented constructively, staff will appreciate and value it. You need to be prepared with examples just in case you are asked for some or what you are saying is doubted.

Scenario

Tiger Woods's childhood golf coach, Ray Andersen, remembers that after each round of golf that Woods played he would not only critique his golf game but would also critique Woods's attitude. He would review each hole with Woods, describing how his attitude influenced his play. He would point out the type of comments Woods would make, his voice tone, and his body position while walking from shot to shot. There seemed to be a direct correlation between Woods's performance and his mood. For example, on the days when Woods would be down on himself for using the wrong club or making an easy error, his score would be higher. When he was more positive and did not let any negativity creep into his game, his score was considerably better. Andersen attributes Woods's greatness not only to his natural and refined skills, but also to his attitude.

STRATEGY 4: ENCOURAGE LAUGHTER OR JOKE LOGS

Suggest to the negativist that he or she keep a log or journal of favorite jokes and when that negativity impulse strikes, take a look at it. It will do wonders. Those frowns will quickly turn to smiles. You can also get the person on a joke-a-day e-mail list or occasionally send him or her a joke over voice mail.

If your whole unit, group, or department comes down with the negativity bug, start a bulletin board with jokes and funny stories. The best joke or story of the day wins a prize. Have people crack up with laughter instead of stress.

Several organizations for which I have consulted have laugh rooms. When a staff member becomes negative or pessimistic, that person is encouraged to leave his or her office and go into a laugh room with hundreds of tapes of popular comedians such as Lily Tomlin, Steve Martin, and Bill Cosby. People put on a tape for ten minutes or so, have a few big laughs, and before they know it, their negative outlook has dissipated. It's great if you can get your team to laugh so hard that they begin to cry. Scientific research has shown that tears of laughter contain an enzyme that, when released, builds up the body's immune system. Laughing can actually be good for you!

SCENARIO

A large book publishing company in the Northeast holds company laugh-ins twice a day. The entire staff downloads one joke at 11:00 a.m. and another at 4:00 p.m. that a staff member was responsible for coming up with for that day. Even the telecommuters and remote staff get involved. On Fridays, it is the chief editor's turn. Instead of jokes, she has to come up with real incidents that happened during that week that will make everyone crack up.

STRATEGY 5: USE THE TAPE RECORDER

Many people's negativity increases or becomes stronger when they have no outlet for expressing how they are feeling about work or what is happening in their personal lives. It would be best if they could speak to a friend or co-worker for a while. Talking often reduces negative feelings and thoughts. Unfortunately, many team members do not have someone to talk to whom they trust or feel comfortable with.

If this is the case for any of your colleagues, suggest that they find themselves a tape recorder and talk into it. They need to release their negativity. Encourage them to really get into it! Tell them that no one is listening. Strategy 5 serves two purposes: The individual has had a chance to express his or her negativity, and after hearing how he or she sounds, the person is much more conscious of future interactions with others. Have the person listen for tone as well as content. Most people cannot believe how negative they are coming across and quickly want to erase their messages.

If there are no tape recorders around, voice mail, fax, or e-mail also work. However, it is always best if the person hears how he or she sounds.

STRATEGY 6: KEEP THOUGHTS IN THE PRESENT

Two other ways some of your teammates get into negativity trouble occur when they use hindsight and anticipation. Hindsight is trying to change what has already happened, which is impossible to do. It is an exercise in futility and is bound to put someone in a negative mood. We have all heard people use hindsight when they have said things like

- "If only I hadn't turned down that transfer."
- "I should have spoken up during the review session."
- "I should have walked out years ago."

Anticipation is worrying about what will happen in the future or situations we have little control over. Staff members may obsess about what a client will say, how many e-mail messages they will have to respond to, or what mood the boss will be in.

Both hindsight and anticipation open the door for the

negativity virus to enter. If your colleagues focus more on the present, they will remain more positive.

STRATEGY 7: HAVE A FAVORITE SAYING

For the past five years I have been doing masters swimming. Masters is for anyone over nineteen who wants to have regularly scheduled workouts with coaches and to remain a competitive swimmer. Last year at an early morning workout I was being very negative.

I was complaining to the coach (Mark Spitz, the winner of the most gold medals in a single Olympics) that I was not getting any faster, that I would never get any faster, and that my strokes were all wrong. I had a few other negative things to say about the water temperature, the other swimmers, and how tired I was. In short, I was having a real strong bout of negativity.

When I finally finished with my tirade, Mark literally pulled me out of the pool and said, "Gary, at least you are in the pool. Imagine how many people could never dream of being in your place." As soon as I heard this, my mood changed. Instead of feeling critical for what I felt were my shortcomings as a swimmer, I realized that I was lucky to be where I was.

At least you're in the pool has now become my favorite saying. It is a phrase that I say to myself whenever I need to get out of a negative, pessimistic state of mind. It puts things back into perspective for me.

Some of my colleagues have shared their favorite phrases with me:

- "I'm in control here."
- "I've got another twenty-four hours to do as much as I can."
- "Wow! I'm alive, and I'm breathing." (This person used to start the day by saying, "I'm exhausted. How will I ever make it through the day?")
- "This is a chocolate mousse—don't sweat it!"

Other people have religious or inspirational sayings, or lines from songs or poems, or quotes from their heroes. The idea is to get your negativist team member to come up with a saying that will wipe away his or her negative thoughts and realize that things are not as bad as the person is making them out to be. The key is that the phrase selected must have a deeply rooted meaning. I also suggest you have people find a saying that they feel is uniquely theirs. That is, one they *believe* is uniquely theirs.

STRATEGY 8: SET A TIME LIMIT FOR NEGATIVITY

Allow your occasional negative people some time to be negative. Give them that luxury.

But when the time limit is up, the negativity ceases. A CEO with whom I work at a major entertainment company in Los Angeles lets his senior staff be as negative as they want to for the first ten minutes of his weekly meeting. After that time period, no negativity is allowed. Another executive at a telecommunications company in Bahrain has five-minute negativity breaks. She gathers up her office staff and allows them this time two or three times a day.

At another organization (and this gets extreme), the manager schedules in on each of his employees' electronic calendars four five-minute negativity meetings a day. Electronically, the staff meets and is allowed to be negative for those periods of time and absolutely no other time during the day.

For some people this may not be enough time. If that is the case where you are, tell staff to be as negative as they want to on the way to work or all day Saturday, but when they approach work, the negativity stops.

STRATEGY 9: SET GROUND RULES

In many organizations, teams or groups set rules on how they want one another to behave at meetings or in the office. These ground rules are usually posted and visible for all to see. This strategy works especially well if the team members come up with the ground rules on their own, not if they are imposed by upper management. When this occurs, the groups take the ownership. It is always much easier to get people to agree to do something when they own it.

Here are some ground rules used in other organizations that may work for your negative team. Their focus is on team meetings.

- "Once a decision has been made, no negativity is allowed."
- "Everyone participates in discussions and gets a turn to voice his or her opinion."

- "We stick to our agenda and our time schedule."
- "When someone comes up with a negative, they must also try to see the positive."
- "We create solutions instead of focusing on problems."
- "When we spot a negative nonverbal or hear negative paralanguage, we tell the person."
- "Negativity costs money. One dollar has to be contributed to the group whenever a negative statement is made." (The money is used to buy dinner for the group.)

STRATEGY 10: SEE THE BIGGER PICTURE— THE 2M APPROACH

Many staff members become negative when they are over-supervised or micromanaged. Others become negative when they do not get the detailed attention they need or are macromanaged. To keep negativity to a minimum, you need to match the amount of support and direction you give your team members with what they need.

Direction is defined as the extent to which you tell people what to do and how to do it, and also the extent to which you make sure your directives are followed. Support is defined as the extent to which you listen to people, encourage and motivate them to do their jobs well.

Some people need a lot of direction or support (they need micromanaging). Others need little direction or support (they need macromanaging). Then there are others who fall somewhere in between. The following descriptions will help you see the connection between what your staff needs from you and whether you manage them in a micro or macro way (the 2M approach).

TEAM MEMBER 1

This is usually a new staff member or someone recently transferred into your group. She seems to be highly motivated but lacks the skills to do well, at least for now. She needs a lot of direction from you. It is OK to micromanage her with the direction, but macromanage with the support.

TEAM MEMBER 2

This person needs large amounts of direction and support. He needs to be micromanaged as well. He has not learned how to do the job yet and seems to be quite discouraged.

TEAM MEMBER 3

This person is an excellent performer and has all the skills to do the job well. She is not that motivated to perform well, however. Perhaps she is bored, does not like the project she is on, has a difficult boss, or is experiencing health or personal problems. She needs high levels of support. Here you would micromanage with the support and macromanage with the direction.

TEAM MEMBER 4

This person is a great performer and also highly motivated to do well as long as you leave him alone. Give him minimal amounts of direction and support. Don't disappear on him, but do not micromanage him!

SCENARIO

Andy Bloom is a team leader at one of the big car manufac-turers. He is currently responsible for a team of seven safety inspectors. One of the inspectors, Damien, has been with the company for eleven years, knows his job very well, and is also very motivated. He fits the description of Team Member 4.

Andy, being new to his position, micromanages Da-mien. He watches him closely, always asks him if he knows what he is doing, and also gives him motivational talks at the beginning of the shift.

This drives Damien bananas. He now spends his day trying to avoid Andy as much as possible. For the first time in eleven years, Damien is feeling negative toward his job. He cannot figure out why he is being so closely supervised when he knows the job much better than Andy does.

STRATEGY 11: LOOK AT QUALITY CRITICISM AS A PLUS

I have seen and heard managers and team members use four different methods of giving performance feedback: being positive, remaining silent, being negative, and ad-dressing quality.

POSITIVE FEEDBACK

As Ken Blanchard said in *The One Minute Manager*, positive feedback is catching people doing something right at work and specifically letting them know what it is and how it has positively influenced the work environment.

Example: "Jon, staying late last week to finish Project K got the deliverable out on time. The customer was very pleased, and we can be assured of a renewal to the contract."

No Feedback

Giving no feedback, either good or bad, is not wise. It leaves people in an unsure and uncertain state and opens the door to negativity.

Example: Jon was conducting a meeting about a redesign of a laptop. He was anxious about his performance because it was his first presentation for the company. No one commented. The boss, who is knowledgeable about the product, just walked away after the meeting and never communicated with Jon.

Negative Feedback

This is when we tell others what they did not do well and offer or ask for no alternative actions (most people become negative when they receive this form of feedback).

Example: "Jon, the customer is distressed with you for not meeting the deliverable date. You really messed up this time."

Quality Feedback

This is when we tell others in specific terms what was not right and what should be done instead or ask them what they would do differently next time.

Example: "Jon, the customer is really distressed with us for not meeting the deliverable date. Tell me what happened and what we could do to prevent this from happening again.''

Positive and quality feedback build a positive work relationship, and negative and silent feedback foster a more negative one, so focus on the former.

STRATEGY 12: COLLECT FUNNY OBJECTS

Another way to reduce a temporarily negative environment is to be prepared with several objects that get others to crack up. When things got too serious or when there was a negativity attack, a former director of customer service at American Express (now a vice president there) would always put on her clown nose and walk through the offices. Everyone would become hysterical, and any negativity that existed at the time was eliminated. In more serious cases she would have to get the individual negativist alone, get him or her in front of a mirror, put the clown nose on that person, and then watch his or her reaction. The smile came, and the negativity vanished.

Other objects that usually reduce negativity include masks, funny glasses, big teeth or fangs.

These objects may also serve many other purposes. For example, the next time you are driving in your car and are trying to merge onto a highway and no one is letting you in, put one of these objects on. What do you think will happen? The other drivers will always let you in!

STRATEGY 13: REENERGIZE WITH IQT

A great strategy that will work for many of your negativists, especially introverted ones, is IQT. Individual quiet time is spending twenty minutes each day alone and without any distractions, thinking of pleasant experiences and places. If done consistently and persistently for at least several weeks, significant mood changes occur.

IQT may not be possible to do at work, and the negativist may have to work on it at home. As mentioned earlier, introverts seem to benefit more from IQT than extroverts. Extroverts get their energy source and drive from other people and from the environment. Quiet, reflective time is not that crucial for them. The introvert, however, must recharge his or her batteries independently. If this opportunity is taken away from introverts, it affects their mood negatively.

A Northern California software design company has IQT every day from 2:00 until 2:20 p.m. No meetings are allowed, no appointments scheduled, phones are put on voice mail, and so on. The CEO and CFO, as well as most of the three hundred staff members, participate. The CEO strongly believes that IQT is a contributing factor to the organization's 28 percent profit margin increase this year.

STRATEGY 14: USE FLIPSIDE THINKING

Getting your team to see the brighter side of things results in their being more positive than negative at work. Have them practice flipside thinking, and their positivism will be on the rise. When a "negative" is threatening to them, have them immediately flip the problem or situation over and look at the positive side. When your team can do this, they will minimize the negative impact that certain situations can have on them.

Let's say that one of your team members has just purchased a new car. What will this person (as well as most new car owners) worry or become negative about for the next several weeks? Correct; this person will agonize over getting that first scratch, dent, or ding. That is why when at the shopping mall or the movie, new car owners will park half a mile away so no other car is parked next to theirs (a prime target for thieves by the way). Now, if you got the team member to use flipside thinking, his or her attitude would be: "I'll throw myself a party when I get that first bang" or "I'll put the first scratch on myself."

Here are some work-related scenarios involving positive thinking:

1. You and your colleagues have just received notice that half the team has been cut from their project and moved to another one.

- Initial Reactions
  "How will we ever complete our project?"
  "They will probably move the rest of us."
  "They are getting ready to get rid of us."
- Flipside Thinking
  "We can take on more responsibilities and learn more."
  "Management feels we can handle it on our own. They have great confidence in our abilities."
  "We will get a greater share of the bonus."

2. Your work hours have been changed from days to nights.

- Initial Reactions
  "It's dangerous being out at night."
  "My body will never be able to adjust."
  "People think much less of night workers."

- Flipside Thinking
  "There'll be no traffic."
  "Get out the surfboard!"
  "No top management will be around."

3. The company is going through its third reorganization this year.

- Initial Reactions
  "I'm going to be downsized."
  "We must be in trouble if they're always reorganizing."
  "Those leaders have no idea what they're doing."
- Flipside Thinking
  "They're finally going to get it right."
  "I'll get a better job in a better department."
  "They're going to get rid of some of the dead weight around here."

Flipside thinking is good practice for shaping positive reactions to change and difficult work situations.

STRATEGY 15: STOP THE THOUGHT!

A very quick technique for stopping a negative thought is to have the person with the negative thought yell out, "Stop thinking that!" If others were around, they would need to yell it to themselves. By doing this, negativity is blocked for a split second. Often the negative thought never comes back. Many sufferers of occasional negativity tell me this is their favorite strategy. It is fast and gets them to quickly refocus. Get your negativists to try it.

SCENARIO

The numbers crunch guy from finance has asked one of your staff to stop by his office. He's going on and on about how your staff member's project is over budget. The staff member begins to think about all the ways she could retaliate against the finance guy for this long harangue. But because you have taught your staff member the thought-stopping technique, she catches herself and uses it. She has refocused and begins to think of constructive solutions to the situation.

STRATEGY 16: WEAR A RUBBER BAND AND SNAP AWAY THE NEGATIVITY

Similar to Strategy 15 but more physical is the rubber band method for eliminating negativity. Give your negative person a rubber band and ask him to wear it on one of his wrists. Tell him that whenever he gets a negative thought he should snap the band. If he does this he will experience some pain, but what else will happen? The negative thought will disappear. It is impossible to experience both the pain and the thought at the same time. If the person is quite negative at the moment, she may need a thicker band, but, on the other hand, we do not want people at work walking around with welts on their wrists. Strategy 16 is a great way for someone to forget her negativity, although it can be somewhat painful.

Of course, if you are feeling negative yourself, you can take a rubber band and snap someone else. This will immediately make you feel more positive.

SCENARIO

Helene is the manager of customer service at a midsize insurance company in Chicago. She used to have a negativity problem there.

Her staff is swamped each day with customers calling up to complain about everything. When the quantity of complaints becomes overwhelming, the staff cannot take it anymore, and they start taking out their negativity on the callers. They even take it out on the phones. They throw the phones to the ground and start kicking them.

Helene realized that neither of these methods was acceptable. She got herself a box of rubber bands and explained the strategy to each of her customer service team members. Now when they get those "difficult" callers, they snap their rubber band, and the negative thoughts they want to share with the caller are forgotten.

STRATEGY 17: USE 3, 2, 1 . . . 1, 2, 3

I have an older brother, Len, who is sometimes very negative. I have tried many strategies with him, but the 3, 2, 1 . . . 1, 2, 3 seems to work best. When I am with him or speak to him on the phone, Len tends to go on and on about how bad things are for him. He can have a long laundry list of everything that is bothering him. When he is done describing in great detail all of the items on the list, I ask him to select the three worst things, then the two worst, and finally, the worst. By doing this I have got him to focus. When they become negative, many people lose the ability to focus. This loss of clarity makes them even more negative.

Then I ask Len to think long and hard and try to come up with one aspect of his life that is fine. When he does this, I ask for two aspects of his life that are fine, and then three, and so on. By using this technique with him, I have changed his thinking paradigm. Len has told me he uses the 3, 2, 1 . . . 1, 2, 3 approach when he has to get himself out of a negative mood.

STRATEGY 18: RESOLVE CONFLICTS—THE WIN-WIN APPROACH

One of the methods to resolve workplace conflicts—collaboration—results in all parties feeling they have won. This method of conflict resolution makes individuals feel more positive. The other four methods—dominate, accommodate, avoid, or compromise—may lead to a bout of negativity. Teach your staff to collaborate when possible. This will prevent a lot of negativity.

SCENARIO

Margot and Alisa are the two floor managers of designer clothes at a leading department store in Dallas. They both possess a great fashion flare but usually differ on what type of displays to use to showcase the latest designs. They have gotten into heated arguments in the past, and the store manager had to step in to resolve their disputes. Neither Margot nor Alisa is ever happy, because the store manager never selects either of their chosen designs. He goes with his own idea.

Eventually the two decided that it would be better to resolve their own conflicts. With the help of the store manager, they learned how to collaborate. In their case, this means coming up with a third option that they can both agree to. They both feel like winners now and are much more positive at work.

STRATEGY 19: SURROUND YOURSELF WITH OPTIMISTIC PEOPLE

Any time you can get a negativist in a room full of optimists, this person's negativity is bound to diminish. He or she actually begins to catch the positive bug. If this is done on a regular basis, the negativist may even begin to develop the behaviors and attitude of the optimists. Remember that the optimists have to be truly optimists. If they are not, the negative person may break down their resistance and make them negative as well. Don't let this great strategy backfire on you.

Optimists may be few and far between in your organization. If this is the case, recommend to the negativist that he try to surround himself with optimistic people outside of work. The same attitude transference will take place this way as well.

A few years ago, I was consulting in an organization that had a very negative culture. The new CEO realized that this attitude was affecting the business. He needed to turn things around quickly. His strategy was to hire extras (actors) to pretend that they were temps. However, they were really there to spread optimism. And it worked!

During World War II, when General Dwight D. Eisenhower was asked what had turned the war around for the Allied forces in Europe, he said that "there is only one

thing that spreads through an organization faster than optimism, and that is pessimism. We, the allied forces, have
been focusing on optimism."

SCENARIO

Ken, a New Orleans investment banker, is constantly
fighting off the negativity of his office mate, Derrick. Derrick bemoans the fact that other brokers are making so
much more than he is. His negativity is well known in the
office, but no one besides Ken is in the direct line of fire
every day. Ken has spoken to his manager about it, but to
no avail. Ken realizes that Derrick's negativity affects his
relationship with the firm's clients, but the manager does
not want to deal with it.

Ken tried many things to make Derrick more positive
at work, but none worked until now. Each morning Ken
has breakfast with a few other bankers, very optimistic
ones. A few weeks ago he insisted that Derrick join them.
He lied about it being a business meeting. At that first
breakfast, Ken noticed a slight attitude change in Derrick.
In the ensuing weeks, Derrick has become much more positive. He has picked up the body language and vocabulary
of the optimistic bankers. Ken has even become more positive. He no longer has to deal with Derrick's ongoing daily
negativity.

STRATEGY 20: BE YOUR OWN BEST FRIEND

When we become negative, we tend to say negative things
to ourselves. We become critical of our mistakes and faults
and say things like, "You idiot! Why did you do that?" or

"What's wrong with you? You messed up again." Think about this. Would you let your best friends say things like this to you? You probably would not. Your team members, when they are in their temporary negative moods, are probably not being their own best friends.

Remind them of this and encourage them to say positive things to themselves.

SCENARIO

A professional colleague of mine, Michael Trent, recently concluded a study he was conducting at the University of Arizona on how self-statements influence attitude and grades. He randomly selected two hundred students to participate in his study. They were all college seniors. One group was instructed to say only positive things to themselves for a six-week period. The other group was given the opposite directions. Michael then compared the two groups on many criteria, such as their attitude toward school, friends, family, and also their grades. He found that the negative statement group had a dimmer view of their relationships and during the course of the study scored 10 percent lower on their exams. He is now writing a paper on the effect of self-statements on academic achievement.

STRATEGY 21: PLAY YOUR WINNERS

Walk around your department or company and look closely at your team members' offices, wall and cubicle spaces, and desks. Do you see pictures of family, friends, pets, or vacation trips? Are diplomas, titles, certificates, awards, or commendations displayed? If the answer is yes to both of these questions, you or your organization allow your people to play their winners all day. You have got them to focus on what they have going for them. This is much better than having them play their losers—and we all have many of them. That is when negativity begins.

I have a staff member, Anthony, who at this point in his life has more losers than winners. He is deeply in debt, has to move out of his house, and is fighting for custody of his son. The two big winners he has going for him are his job and his completing his MBA. I have him focus on his winners as much as possible to build his positive attitude. Anthony's challenge, as well as mine as his boss, is to get him to push his losers to the outer boundaries of his thinking.

Here are a few techniques to help you get your team to play their winners:

- Have them talk about their winners to you and others. When they do this, these winners become even more important to them.
- Have them make a list of their winners and keep it where they can see it. Anthony has his list on his computer screen. It is the first and last thing he sees at work each day.
- Make it a habit to remind your team of their skills, accomplishments, and strengths.
- Share team, department, and company successes with them.
- Have solution-creating sessions with your team on how they can make some of their losing work situations into winners.

STRATEGY 22: PROVIDE A NEW OPPORTUNITY OR SKILL

Many individuals get temporary bouts of negativity at work when they feel stuck in their jobs. A great way to get them out of this mood is to provide them with a new learning opportunity or skill. They will immediately begin to feel better. It is always best to allow the person to decide what he or she would like to learn.

SCENARIO

Chris has been an analyst at one of the big accounting firms for two years, having been recruited right out of college. He has become quite proficient in his job as a proposal writer. He has several friends in other firms in similar positions. They tell him how they are expanding into other areas and are updating their skills.

Chris is not experiencing this at his firm, and it is beginning to cause him to become negative. He believes he will not be marketable unless he keeps developing his skills.

He has spoken to management about it, but they say they have no other learning opportunities for him at the moment. Chris has told management that he is strongly thinking about looking elsewhere, as developing marketable skills is very important to him. The company understands Chris's growth needs and offered him a position with another division in Europe. Chris is almost certain that he will take the new assignment.

STRATEGY 23: DO SOMETHING TO HELP OTHERS

Quite often, a team member's negativity is driven by his or her self-focus. If we can switch people's focus away from themselves and onto something else, their negativity will diminish. One of the best ways to accomplish this is to get your negativist to help other people, whether at work or outside of work. Many organizations have mentoring programs in which the staff is assigned newer members to help "show them the ropes." Many others are now getting their work done by teams in which the more experienced employees help the less experienced ones.

Other companies actually give their staff time off to do volunteer or community service work. They call these days Developing Others Days. Studies have shown that when people return to work after such service, they are much more optimistic, and their productivity increases as well.

STRATEGY 24: THE AAA APPROACH

The AAA approach—alter, avoid, and accept—can reduce people's feelings of powerlessness at work by getting them to realize that they truly have choices, even though they may not be the optimal choices. Let's say your colleague Della has a boss from hell. Whenever she sees, hears, or thinks about her boss she gets a negativity attack. The boss is making Della's life miserable, and she does not believe she can do anything about it. You need to familiarize Della with the AAA approach. She has choices. She is not powerless in this situation.

ALTER

Della could try to alter the situation by speaking to her boss or getting advice from colleagues or human resources on how to handle the situation, or she could look at her own work behaviors that may be in conflict with her boss's and try to alter some of them.

AVOID

Della could make believe there is no problem and just not deal with it.

ACCEPT

You could have Della realize that if *she chooses* to work here, this is who the boss is going to be, at least for the time being.

I suggest that the next time one of your teammates is feeling trapped, review the AAA approach with them. People need to understand that they have options and then decide which option would be best.

STRATEGY 25: REWARD YOURSELF FOR BEING POSITIVE

One of the best ways to get your negativists to practice being positive is to have them reward themselves. The rewards could be as simple as taking themselves out to lunch, buying themselves a small present, or seeing that movie, play, or concert that they were depriving themselves of. Of course, you could also throw in a few rewards yourself. Besides giving them some positive feedback (which works wonders), you could take them out for coffee, let them leave a little earlier one day, or give them that new project they were asking for.

SCENARIO

Fred was a real negative guy at work. He was always upset with the way his projects turned out. He would also criticize the work of his teammates as never being good enough. Marcia, Fred's project leader, noticed Fred's behaviors and the impact they had on him and the rest of the crew. Marcia also noticed that when she gave Fred some feedback for being positive, he responded much more favorably than when she criticized his negative behaviors. After a good day, she would occasionally spring for a beer or tell him to leave a little earlier. Fred soon got the message that being positive was the way to go.

Marcia did not view these "rewards" as payoffs. She looked at them as a return on investment. When she showed her appreciation for a positive attitude, she got high productivity. If these rewards did not work, she was not going to raise the stakes and bribe Fred. She would have to hold him accountable for his negativity.

Marcia is now working on having Fred notice the change in his behavior and having him take some of the responsibility for rewarding himself. She believes that Fred will eventually take most of the responsibility.

STRATEGY 26: LOCK IN THE NEGATIVITY AT WORK

I have always admired people who, no matter how negative their workplace or how many negative people they have working alongside of them, are able to leave the negativity at work and go on with their lives. They are able to lock in the negativity at work and not allow it to affect their attitudes for the rest of the day.

After some trial and error, I have found a few strategies that enable me to do the same. Several clients recommended the methods that I now use.

At the end of the day, one of my clients records all the day's negative occurrences and the negative comments he has heard and locks them in his credenza, saying, "I'll be back; don't go anywhere." Another client, who is a single mother, has a baseball cap in her car that says "Mom" on it. When she leaves the office and gets in her car, she puts on the cap. She has focused on something else. This lets her tune out the day's negativity.

A third client tells me that he and his wife have a pact never to talk about work at home unless they have positive things to say. Other clients go to the gym, play tennis, swim, do yoga, or bicycle. These activities serve two purposes. First, they greatly help people take their minds off their negative workplaces. Second, they enable people to build up their immune systems to fight the negativity bug.

The strategy I like best, however, was recently told to me at an executive seminar I was conducting for an organization that has an extremely high level of negativity. The executive said that it is not leaving the office that separates him from the negativity, nor is it the drive home, the walking into his house, the opening of the refrigerator door, or the procurement of the bottle of beer. It is, though, the clicking sound that the bottle cap makes. That does it for him. No more negativity.

Have a discussion with your staff, especially those who seem to take the negativity with them when they leave work. Ask them to come up with a few strategies for locking it in or suggest a few to them. When people are able to lock in the negativity at work, they seem to enjoy the rest of their lives more. When they do this, the negative workplace does not have such a devastating impact on them.

STRATEGY 27: ASSIGN NUMBERS TO CERTAIN WORDS

Warning: Use with discretion!

Assigning numbers to curse words is a great strategy. But before you share it with your negative people, determine whether it would be OK to recommend it in your workplace. Here is how it works.

Have your negativists think of all of their curse words. Then have them write them down and assign a number to each one. When your negativists find themselves in a situation that is bound to cause negativity or stress, they can say "14," "11," or "8." When they see that difficult colleague or boss or customer who usually just sets them off, they can say to themselves "3," "7," or "19."

SCENARIO

Jamie works at the help desk in a very fast-paced computer graphics company in the Silicon Valley. Her internal clients are exceptionally demanding. They need things yesterday. The clients often are very demeaning and gruff toward anyone working the desk.

Jamie always has her list with her. She has actually assigned certain numbers to certain people. For example, Don, the sarcastic engineer who believes that the company would be nothing without its engineers and that help desk people are a dime a dozen, gets number 5. When Jamie sees his number come on her screen, she writes down a big 5 on her notepad and has a few chuckles. Don's actions no longer cause her to have a negativity attack.

STRATEGY 28: USE THE STANDING OVATION

Often our teammates complain, criticize, or tell others how bad they have it. I know I have done it, and I am sure you have as well. Have your colleagues think about the reaction they get. I am sure it is not a positive one. They get frowned on, criticized back, or ignored. This in turn probably makes them even more negative.

It would be much better if they could walk in at the beginning of a meeting and say, "It was really difficult getting here on time, but I made it. I would like a standing ovation." Or, "I just spent one hour placating Mr. Y [the most difficult customer]. I need a standing ovation."

The standing ovation also works in reverse. For example, when a coworker is seen struggling through a tough project or handling a challenging employee, give him a standing ovation. If a customer unjustifiably chewed out a colleague, gather a few coworkers and give the colleague a standing ovation. It makes people feel so much better.

The reactions to the standing ovation will be amazing. Morale and team spirit will rise. Start clapping at work.

STRATEGY 29: TAKE SOME PICTURES

The adage "a picture paints a thousand words" couldn't be truer when you are trying to cure those temporary bouts of negativity. What you do here, preferably with people's permission, is take some pictures of your staff or colleagues in their offices, at meetings, while sitting in the cafeteria, and so forth and then show them the pictures (you can even make videotapes).

Many people would never believe that they were coming across as negative. When they see their body language in the pictures, however, they become convinced. Remember we said that body language accounts for or plays the largest part in how others perceive our attitude.

SCENARIO

Hank did not realize that he was spreading negativity at his not-for-profit organization in Washington, D.C. He never smiled, he walked hunched over, and he sighed much of the time. At meetings, either his hands covered his face or he would pull his hair, and he constantly fidgeted.

When Hank's staff (fortunately he has a great one) pointed out his nonverbal behaviors to him at a party one evening, he was in total denial. The staff explained that they were beginning to feel negative at work because they always got the sense, based on Hank's body language, that he was uninterested or did not care about the organization's mission. The staff asked Hank if they could demonstrate their point by photographing him. He agreed. The rest is history.

STRATEGY 30: BUY SOME WHIPS

Warning: Use with discretion!

Some negativists like to cause pain for themselves by

taking the blame for things out of their control or putting themselves down for being inadequate. Many other negativists just like to complain about things: the weather, their colleagues, their family, the cafeteria, even the time of day. I am sure you are getting the picture. These negativists like to be punished.

If this sounds all too familiar, I suggest you go to an equestrian shop and buy a few small whips. Hand them out to the negativists just described. Tell them to always have their whips handy because they may never know when they will need them.

They may need them on mornings when it's raining and they know it will take twice as long to get to work. Tell them to give themselves a couple of lashes.

They may need them when they stop at Starbucks on the way to work and find that the store has run out of their favorite blend of coffee. Tell them to give themselves a couple of lashes.

Or they may need them at the next staff meeting when the boss starts to talk about the next reorganization. Tell them to give themselves a few lashes.

Negativists can learn a lot from these whips. They will soon see how irrational and self-defeating their behavior is. You can even suggest to them that they lend the whips to other people in the office who are acting negatively and pessimistically.

SCENARIO

Theresa runs one of the largest not-for-profit agencies in Los Angeles. The work is hard, the staff put in long hours, and the pay is much less than that of the private sector. Theresa gets some negativity, but she is usually able to manage it. She did have one entire department, however, that came down with the negativity bug.

Theresa tried the whip strategy, and it worked splendidly for her. At the annual holiday party she gave each staff member in this department a little whip. She put foam rubber on the tips of the whips so that no one would get hurt. She explained that the whips were to be used whenever someone was acting in a negative way or saying something negative. This person would have to give himself or herself a few lashes. The idea was that because people were beating themselves up anyway, why not actually have them do it?

After a couple of weeks of using the whips (the staff monitored one another to make sure everyone played by the rules), the negativity ceased. They had learned their lesson in a very dramatic way.

Theresa still has the whips, and she uses them whenever she needs to manage someone's negativity. The staff has learned the futility of punishing themselves.

SUMMARY

Chapter 3 provided you with thirty strategies for managing negativity. Even though many of the techniques seem a little out of the box, they definitely work! The main idea behind many of these techniques is to get your negative people to lighten up—to not take themselves so seriously.

Chapter 4

DEALING WITH PERVASIVE INDIVIDUAL AND TEAM NEGATIVITY

In this chapter we talk about how to handle severe cases of individual or team negativity. The method we use, the accountability model, gives you a step-by-step process for confronting individuals or teams whose negativity is ongoing and affects their work, the work of others, or the organization in a serious way.

For the moment we will put aside the objective of managing negativity to focus on how to confront it, demand that it change, and document it. We must consider negativity as a bottom-line business issue that needs to be confronted in much the same way that performance and other behavior problems are confronted.

BEHAVIOR PROBLEMS

Examples of behavior problems include the following:

- Time abuse: lateness, excessive absences, being missing in action
- Inappropriate dress, choice of words
- Rudeness toward customers
- Excessive socialization (I once worked with a guy who thought his major job function was to run the company football pool)
- Negativity: disagreeing with management, putting down decisions, constant arguing, and so on

Managers and team leaders seem much more hesitant to address behavior problems than performance ones. Their justifications seem to adhere to the following logic:

1. Behavior problems come too close to someone's personality, and we all know that we cannot try to change that.
2. Behavior problems are not as easily documented as performance ones.
3. Behavior problems really do not affect work performance, and we just have to learn to live with difficult, negative people.

There is much truth to the first two points. As we already know, one's personality has a great influence on how our attitudes are shaped, and we never want to try to change personality, just behavior. Also, documenting performance problems is probably easier than documenting behavioral ones.

The third point, however, is definitely not true. Ongoing negativity and other behavior problems are serious; if not addressed, they will affect the business or organization.

Still, clients often tell me that some of their most negative people or people with other behavior problems are their best performers. They ask me why they have to deal with behavior problems. For example, Barry, a manager at a Southern California utility company, has a very negative team member, Jenny. When he confronted her negativity, she replied, "You may be right about my attitude, but at least I work around here. In fact, I do twice as much as anybody else." He thought about Jenny's reply, knew she was right, and dropped the confrontation.

Was he correct in doing that?

If he could answer no to all of the following three questions, then he (or anybody else faced with behavior problems) was right in dropping the confrontation:

1. Is her negativity affecting her work performance?
2. Is her negativity affecting the performance of others?
3. Is her negativity affecting the organization or its bottom line in some way?

I have found that 98 percent of behavior problems, including negativity, can be given a yes answer to one or more of the preceding questions. In Barry's case, Jenny's negativity does affect the performance of others. Jenny's teammates find the work environment unpleasant, as conflicts are always arising. This affects their morale, which in turn affects their productivity negatively. Barry must confront Jenny's negativity just as he would have to confront any other behavior or performance problem that affects the business.

HOW TO CONFRONT CONSTANT NEGATIVITY

The Accountability Model

Let's say that you have tried to be supportive and understanding. You have looked the other way. You have tried all thirty recommended strategies from Chapter 3 plus a few of your own. You have yelled, screamed, shouted, and even begged. Nothing has worked. Your negativist is as negative as ever. If this is the case, you have no other choice but to hold the person accountable for his or her negativity.

Here's how to do it. (Note the similarities between the accountability model introduced here and the twenty-one consecutive days model from Chapter 2.)

Step 1

Focus on the behavior(s), not the personality, of the individual. It is very difficult to change a person's personality and you are not professionally qualified to do so. It is much more reasonable to plan on changing unacceptable behaviors.

Step 2

In specific terms, identify the negative behavior(s) and its (their) impact. Remember, if there is no impact on performance, morale, customers, productivity, and so on, then there is no problem.

Step 3

Wait for the negativist's response. He or she may finally own up to it, and it will be much easier to fix. Also, there may be some legitimate reason for the person's negativity that you were not aware of. Perhaps you could do something about it. Keep in mind, even at this time of confrontation, that you are still trying to change behavior. Your view should not be that you are out to get this person.

Step 4

Identify alternative actions or behaviors that the negativist needs to take and point out the consequences if not taken. Offer the negativist special services provided by the organization such as the employee assistance program or counseling. Some negativists may not be capable of changing on their own and will need special help.

This step is the key to the accountability model. If the negativist does not follow the action plan developed during this step, you need to take a more serious action, such as discipline.

It is always best if the negativist comes up with the suggestion for change. If that occurs, we get their ownership. Many studies have shown that people will much more readily do something if they came up with the answer or plan. Keep in mind, however, that many negativists may not know what to do differently or will not want to contribute to this action-planning step. You need to take the lead in those situations.

Step 5

Monitor the behavior and give feedback. If the behavior improves, give positive feedback; if it doesn't, follow your organization's discipline procedure. Negativity is a business issue. One may have to be terminated for it.

CASE STUDY: THE CENTER FOR MANAGEMENT

Several years ago I was the director of new products at a Manhattan-based consulting firm, the Center for Management. One of my staff members at the time, Helene, an instructional design specialist, was an incredible performer. Her skills, abilities, and knowledge of the field were excellent, as were her finished assignments. This may sound hard to believe, but I had to fire Helene.

Helene was a negativity carrier. She would usually complain about the work performance of her peers. She would belittle their projects, their capabilities, and their work effort. She also showed her negativity by telling me, and others, that my boss, the CEO, was making wrong decisions and did not know what direction to take the company.

The staff, especially her fellow instructional designers, would come to me disgruntled. They believed Helene was affecting their performance by bringing down their morale and their commitment to their jobs. They began to question their capabilities and those of the CEO. After a time I noticed that they, too, began to become negative.

I tried many things to manage Helene's negativity. I would try to lift her spirits by using many of the strategies we have already talked about—3, 2, 1, . . . 1, 2, 3; flipside thinking; rubber band; standing ovation; funny glasses; and so forth. They did not work. The rest of the staff tried other strategies. They did not work. During two performance review sessions (we did them quarterly), I talked to Helene about how her "attitude" (of course, I was very specific) was affecting the performance of others. I explained that it needed to change and offered outside assistance if she wanted it. She changed for about a week after the discussion, and then the negative behaviors returned.

To be honest, I probably waited a bit too long to address Helene's negativity with her. I overlooked her negativity because she was such a great performer—the best on my staff of eight.

Finally, I realized that I had no other choice but to confront her negativity and used the accountability model as my guide. I focused on only her negative behaviors. I was very specific in describing these behaviors and the impact that they were having on others. I made it a business issue.

Helene found it hard to accept some of these impact statements. When this occurred, I gave her some examples—actual work-related situations—of her behaviors and their impact on others. I tried to get Helene to agree that it was important to change. I do not think she bought in to it.

I next outlined what behaviors I needed from Helene instead. For example, I told her that, rather than criticize her colleagues' projects and belittle their efforts, she should not make any comments. I also told her to watch her nonverbal behaviors, like the frown on her face when a colleague, Lamar, would give us an update on his progress at a staff meeting. It was very difficult to get as specific as I did, but I realized it was the only way that I would be able to monitor Helene's change in behavior.

I then had to point out the consequences. I told Helene that if I did not see a change in all the behaviors that we had just discussed within two weeks and that if these new behaviors did not replace the old ones permanently, I would have to start a discipline procedure, which could result in termination.

I realized that my being so direct could cause Helene to become even more negative and even affect her high level of performance. I had to take the risk and accept that this might occur.

Two weeks later I had a follow-up meeting with Helene. I gave her some positive feedback on a couple of behaviors that seemed to improve but expressed regrets that most of the others had not. Because I did not see a significant change in her negativity, I had to begin the company's discipline procedure.

The first step was to put my observations in writing and show them to Helene. She had the option of signing or refusing to do so. She refused.

Unfortunately, Helene's negativity continued. The discipline procedure also began to affect other behaviors that before had been perfect—punctuality and attendance. In addition, her performance slipped. It took about eight months of continual documentation and progressive discipline before I could terminate Helene.

I still have regrets about what I did. The organization lost a great instructional designer.

When I put things into perspective, however, I realize that no individual, no matter how excellent his or her performance, comes above the norms or required behaviors of an organization. We lost Helene, but the staff's morale and productivity increased.

This is an extreme case (the termination, that is), but I have used it to demonstrate that negativity may have to be taken very seriously. The good news is that such situations rarely get to the termination stage. You should address pervasive and ongoing negativity as soon as you recognize that it is having an impact on the performance of that person, others, or on the organization. When you wait too long, the message is that you are condoning this kind of behavior, and it becomes much more difficult to change.

HOLDING A TEAM ACCOUNTABLE FOR THEIR NEGATIVITY

You may one day be in the position of having to confront the negativity of an entire team. The accountability model works just as well for teams as it does for individuals. Here are a few pointers for use with teams:

1. Don't blame the entire team for the negative behaviors or unacceptable performance issues of one or some of its members. Hold those members accountable, not the team. Holding the team accountable can make positive team members more negative.

2. Do not wait too long to bring up the negative behaviors. If you do, the team will get the message that their behaviors really aren't that important. After all, why did you wait so long to address them?

3. As I discuss in the next section, team negativity may have to do with organizational causes. A much better

strategy (and one with great long-term results) is to address these organizational causes. You will have to do much less confronting. If this is not possible, the team's negative behaviors must still be confronted.

CASE STUDY: THE REFURBISHING TEAM

I am currently consulting for a firm that does hotel renovations. I have been working with one of their project teams—the team in charge of guestroom refurbishing (putting in new furniture, carpeting, draperies, and so forth). The organization is a pretty positive place to work. Most of the other teams (it is a team-based organization) appear to be very satisfied, and their managers or team leaders attest to that. The refurbishing team, however, is rather negative. They show their negativity by privately and publicly ridiculing the organization. They are critical of the leaders and the other teams and are constantly complaining about how difficult their jobs are. The company is afraid that the overt negativity of this team may begin to influence other teams.

Let's work through the accountability model and demonstrate how to use the steps with a negative team. Keep in mind that this is the final approach to managing negativity: confronting it. Let's assume that many of the other strategies that would precede confrontation did not work, or the company was unable to redress the issues that are causing the team's negativity.

USING THE ACCOUNTABILITY MODEL FOR TEAMS

STEP 1

Focus on the team members' behaviors, not their personalities. Here the negative behavior is complaining about the organization in front of clients and other staff members. The refurbishing team complains about how they get treated, how the other teams are more valued than they are, and how their leader doesn't respect them or treat them as well as the other teams.

Step 2

Identify the negative behaviors in specific terms and describe their impact. The behaviors are described in Step 1; their impacts include the following:

- The clients are getting an unfavorable opinion of the company.
- Other teams avoid the refurbishing team when they need to work together.
- There is a reduction in the team's work performance.
- Positive new team members are being converted into negative ones.

Step 3

Wait and listen to their response. Team members may have justifiable reasons for feeling negative (lower salary than the other teams, no input into decision-making, an impossible boss, and so on). Correcting these problems would be ideal, but this may not always be possible. You can still expect people to behave in a certain way, and if they don't, you need to hold them accountable.

Step 4

Initiate action planning. Here the confronters (in this case, senior management) and the team work together to devise a plan of action to change the team's negative behaviors. It is also during this action step that the consequences for not changing are presented. In the case of the refurbishing team, the action plan was as follows:

- There will be no more complaining in public, only through appropriate channels.
- A positive working relationship will be built with the other teams.

Very specific new behaviors were developed to meet these two overall goals. The consequence established for not changing was suspension without pay.

STEP 5

Monitor the change in behavior and give feedback. The team succeeded and became much more positive. They were given positive feedback for their improvement. Two things enabled this transformation. First, the confronters were serious. They would not accept the team's negativity. They were willing to dismiss each team member if necessary. Second, the confronters realized that the team had some legitimate complaints and began to address them. Discipline was never needed, and the team is performing at a much higher level than before they were held accountable for their negativity.

It is usually more challenging to hold a team accountable than an individual, but the same confrontation strategy must be applied.

NEGATIVITY AND PATHOLOGY

It has been estimated that approximately 1 to 2 percent of individuals at work (or in the general population) are constantly negative. That means that they cannot control their negative reactions or behaviors and need special help. The help can come in the form of therapy or medication. Clinical depression would be an example of a condition that could cause someone to be pathologically negative.

The techniques used in this book may not work with these individuals. You are also not qualified to "treat" them. Please refer them to your employee assistance program or to the appropriate resource.

In addition, we cannot be expected to provide counseling to team members with serious problems such as substance abuse or family problems that are the cause of their severe negativity. In such cases, it is best to make a referral.

However, you, as the manager or team leader, can and should provide a supportive environment so that an unhappy teammate feels free to express himself or herself. Once the underlying causes are understood, it is possible to work together toward a solution that will prevent attacks of negativity and make the team member more productive.

SUMMARY

Please do not avoid the accountability model. Remember that you may have no other choice but to confront the negativist and hold that person accountable for changing his or her behaviors. Too many people avoid it because it is a lot of work. The results, however, are worth it.

Section II

MAJOR CAUSES AND CURES FOR ORGANIZA- TIONAL NEGATIVITY

Chapter 5

CHANGE AND NEGATIVITY

In this chapter I discuss how continual change is one of the major causes of organizational negativity. I talk about how to reduce people's resistance to change, thus reducing their negativity. The VISAR model guarantees that resistance gets reduced. I look at people's various reactions to change and the organization's role in increasing support for change.

I also introduce a strategy for determining if the time is right for the organization to make a change. Finally, I explore the correlation between change, risk, and negativity.

Many CEOs and company leaders with whom I have worked during the past several years have told me that, even in these excellent economic times, negativity is on the increase in their organizations. They point to rapid and continuous change as one of the leading causes of this negativity.

It is not change itself, but rather how companies introduce and manage the change, that results in a negative or positive acceptance of it. For example, at a 3,000-employee manufacturing company in the South-west (let's call it NT, Inc.), most of the workforce responded quite negatively to a new computer system. On the surface, it seemed that they were displeased with the system itself. But with further investigation, it turned out to be the way the change was handled that led to their negativity.

NT just sprang the change on the entire staff. After a three-day weekend, the staff walked in and found their old computers gone, replaced by the new ones. They were quite annoyed and soon became very negative about this change. They were not aware that the change was taking place, they missed their old system, they could think of no reason why they were changing computers, and they did not know the intricacies of this new system.

It is normal for people to resist change, and there are many reasons for this resistance. The company's role is to try to reduce this resistance, not eliminate it (which is impossible). The more that resistance to change is reduced, the more positive people will be about change.

First, let's take a look at the reasons why people resist change.

- They are uncertain of what the new change will bring.
- They are used to doing something one way; it is difficult to change.
- They believe that the current way of doing things is fine and cannot understand why a change is necessary.
- They feel that top management may not know what they are doing; they do not trust the "flavor of the month."

- They have had unfortunate experiences with change—getting downsized, relocation, new boss, and so on.
- They have experienced the 3 C's—loss of control, loss of community, and loss of competence (from Chapter 1).
- They are afraid that the change will be the catalyst for the loss of their job.

THE VISAR

Some of these reasons for resisting change were present at NT, Inc. The leadership of the organization could have done something about these resisting factors. They could have planned the change using the VISAR, a method of managing change that dramatically reduces negativity toward change. The more of the five VISAR elements accounted for, the more positive the change experience will be. The more positive people are about change, the less negativity that will exist.

The five elements for successful change (VISAR) are as follows:

1. Vision. The better people understand the reasons for a change, the more they will remain positive about it.

2. Incentives. If individuals realize that a change will benefit them or the organization, negativity subsides.

3. Skills. People become anxious—and anxious people become negative—when they feel they lack the skills needed to perform.

4. Action Plan. Individuals like to know the specific steps involved in a change. The more they know about how it will be implemented, the more positive they remain.

5. Resources. Staff members need time, tools, money, and other resources to implement change in a positive manner.

If you are missing one or more of the VISAR elements in a change effort, the consequences will be negative. As shown in Table 5-1, the result can range from confusion to frustrations.

Confusion

If there is no vision, people get confused during the change process. They say things like "Why are we doing this? Do they really think this is wise?" or simply "Why do we have

Table 5-1: The Five Ingredients for Successful Change: The VISAR

Items					*Result*	
Vision	Incentives	Skills	Action Plan	Resources	=	Change
	Incentives	Skills	Action Plan	Resources	=	Confusion
Vision		Skills	Action Plan	Resources	=	Change Too Gradual
Vision	Incentives		Action Plan	Resources	=	Anxiety
Vision	Incentives	Skills		Resources	=	False Start
Vision	Incentives	Skills	Action Plan		=	Frustration

to change?'' Rumors are often prevalent when the vision is not communicated. People spread rumors because they need information. When there is no information, they need to create their own information. Provide the reasons for the change, and there will be less negativity and confusion.

CHANGE TOO GRADUAL

If there are no incentives for change, people will not want to do it. You will have to force them to change. When this occurs, the change will be implemented too slowly. Slow-paced change may no longer be appropriate for most organizations today. When you point out the benefits of the change—acquisition of new skills, more marketable products or services, increased customer satisfaction—people will understand its necessity and have the motivation to implement it.

ANXIETY

To prevent the negative consequence of the third element of the VISAR, anxiety, provide individuals with the training experiences they need. It may mean to further their education, provide classes, or do one-on-one coaching.

FALSE STARTS

To prevent a lot of false starts, have a carefully thought-out action plan and then communicate it to everyone involved with the change. This ensures that the change will be more successful and that it gains the staff's support and confidence.

FRUSTRATION

Without the necessary resources, there is frustration. Negativity really sets in when people have bought into the change, are prepared for it, and have the incentive, skills, and abilities but are not provided the adequate resources.

PEOPLE'S REACTIONS TO CHANGE

People have five different reactions to change. The specific change situation usually determines one's reaction. However, there also seems to be an automatic response for most people when they just hear the word *change* at work, even before they know exactly what the change is. Let's look at the five reactions that people have to change.

1. They become joiners.
2. They become receptors.
3. They become neutrals.
4. They become passive resisters.
5. They become active resisters.

JOINERS

These people immediately encourage the change. They talk it up, volunteer to do anything to make it work, and actively enlist the support of others. The word *active* is the key here. Joiners are not necessarily formal leaders; they often come from the rank and file. In fact, as many leadership theories attest to, informal leaders often have more influence in organizational life than the formal ones. Joiners are very positive, and their can-do attitude infects others.

RECEPTORS

These people are willing to accept the change and see positive aspects to it. They work hard to implement the change and hope it succeeds. However, they do not promote it or encourage others to support it.

NEUTRALS

These people neither like nor dislike the change. If it were up to them, they would rather not have to change. But if the boss or organization expects them to implement the change, they will. They often have an emotionless reaction to change and are basically resigned to it.

PASSIVE RESISTERS

These people do not like the change and do not want to implement it. But they show their resistance in a passive way. They may talk up the change but then just not do it. They may do it half-heartedly or haphazardly. Passive resisters fear conflict, disagreement, and showing opposition. In short, they do not like the change and will try not to make it work—but you do not know this until after the fact. They may show their passive-aggressiveness by, for example, going into the new computer system that they opposed and sabotaging its operation.

ACTIVE RESISTERS

Like passive resisters, active resisters do not like the change and do not want to implement it. However, the active ones are aggressive about their resistance. They may speak against it at meetings or with their colleagues or teams. They are very open about their view of the change and adamantly oppose it. They may even refuse to implement or support the change and actively enlist others to do the same. Losing their jobs or getting ostracized is of little concern to them.

My organization, SilverStar Enterprises, has been conducting research into people's reactions to the word *change*, and we have come up with findings that explain why some organizations may be more negative than others. The results of our studies on reaction to change indicate the following:

1. As already mentioned, there is a direct correlation between people's reactions to change and what the change is. For example, during a recent reorganization at an oil refinery company in Houston, a manager became a joiner. She was informed that both her department and her budget would double in size. A few weeks later, however, when she was told that her entire staff (now more than seventy-five) would have to be trained on a new procedural system that she was highly opposed to, she became an active resister.

2. Joiners and receptors have a more positive attitude at work, and their attitude seems to spread to others. Resisters, both passive and aggressive, seem to have a more negative attitude that gets communicated to others. Neutrals are somewhere along the middle of the continuum (see Figure 5-1).

3. People in the workplace can alter their reactions to change (see Figure 5-2). That is, for example, most neutrals,

if the change is handled well (using the VISAR elements), can move up the model and become receptors or even joiners. If the change is not handled well by the organization, these same neutrals can move down the model and become resisters. Along these same lines, when change is not implemented well, joiners or receptors become neutrals or even resisters; if the change is implemented well, resisters become neutrals or may even move way up the model and become receptors or joiners.

Our research leads us to believe that it is not the individuals within the organization who determine their level of resistance, but it is how the change is handled—vision and communication, incentives, skill preparation, action plan, resources—by the organization and its leaders that determines individuals' level of resistance.

Organizations and their leaders and managers have the key role in reducing resistance to change. They need to do the following:

- Involve the staff in the change—ask them for their active participation. This leads to ownership and commitment.

- Communicate often and clearly the purpose for the change.

Figure 5-1

The Negative-Positive Continuum

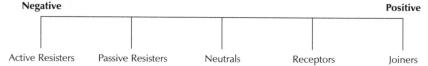

- Communicate exactly what is expected from the implementers of the change—leave no surprises.
- Break the change down into manageable steps.
- Be a model. Demonstrate your commitment to the change.
- Celebrate successes.
- Honor the past and do not badmouth the way things used to be.
- And of course, remember the VISAR elements for successful change.

THE THREE-STAGE PROCESS (BENEFITS VERSUS RESISTERS ANALYSIS)

As we already know, negativity increases if change is not handled well. Negativity also increases if change does not succeed; that is, was the change a mistake in the first place? To prevent the latter from occurring, managers need to analyze whether the change makes sense or, in other terms, if its benefits outweigh the resisting factors. The three-stage process for determining whether to proceed with a change (adapted from the research of the Drieford Group) enables

Figure 5-2

Changing Reactions to Change Model

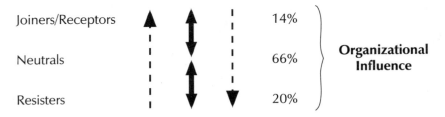

Joiners/Receptors	14%	
Neutrals	66%	Organizational Influence
Resisters	20%	

managers to determine if a prospective change makes sense.

At first glance, the process will seem pretty simplistic. It is important to keep in mind, however, that much detailed work needs to go into the process when it is being used with a real change situation.

STAGE 1: DETERMINE THE CHANGE'S OVERALL BENEFITS

During this stage the manager needs to decide on what the benefits of the change are. He or she should enlist the help of others by forming a change team. Examples of benefits include increased profits and sales, customer and employee satisfaction, faster deliverable times, and so on. Then based on the specific benefits identified, the manager (team) would evaluate the change's overall level of benefit (see Figure 5-3) for the group or department. It is always best to quantify these benefits into profits or savings.

STAGE 2: DETERMINE THE OVERALL RESISTANCE TO THE CHANGE

The manager (team) then determines all of the factors that would prevent the change from working—the resisting factors. Examples of these include time, money, governmental

Figure 5-3

Level of Overall Benefit

Low 0   Moderate 50   High 100

restraints, environmental concerns, staff training and education costs, and so forth. Then, based on the specific resistance factors identified, the manager (team) would evaluate the overall level of resistance (see Figure 5-4) that the change will encounter. It is always best to quantify these resisting factors into costs or dollars.

STAGE 3: DETERMINE WHETHER TO IMPLEMENT THE CHANGE

Here the manager (team) analyzes whether to proceed with the change by plotting the overall benefit and resistance numbers onto the "Proceed with Change?" graph (see Figure 5-5).

Let's work through an actual case to demonstrate the three-step process.

CASE STUDY: THE BIOCHEMICAL DEPARTMENT MOVE

Marcie Rutherford, the manager of the chemical engineering department at a 375-employee biotech research and development company in Southern California, is considering moving her biochemical engineering department sixty miles from the main campus to a site of its own in San Diego. Rapid growth (the need for additional space) and difficulty in recruiting biochemical engineers are the driving forces for the change. Marcie believes that a new state-of-the-art facility in a desirable and convenient location would retain

Figure 5-4

Level of Overall Resistance

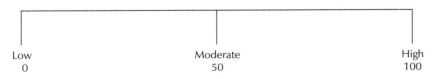

Low	Moderate	High
0	50	100

Figure 5-5

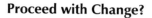

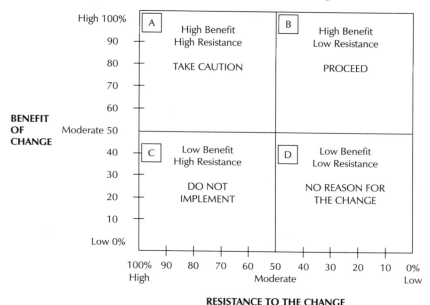

current staff members and attract new ones. Marcie's boss asked her to conduct the three-step process to determine whether to proceed with this change.

Stage 1: Determine the Change's Overall Benefits

Some of the major benefits Marcie and the cross-functional team working with her came up with are as follows:

1. Increased morale for the biochemists (state-of-the-art facility)
2. Proximity to a major city and international airport
3. Attraction of new candidates

After a very careful and detailed analysis, they agreed that the overall benefit of the change was high, around an 80. (See Figure 5-6.)

Figure 5-6

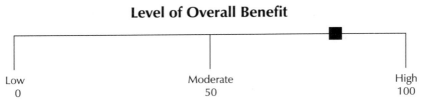

Level of Overall Benefit

Low   Moderate   High
0   50   100

Stage 2: Determine the Overall Resistance to the Change

Some of the strong resisting factors Marcie and the change team came up with are as follows:

1. Relocation costs for current biochemical engineers
2. Housing costs would be much more expensive
3. Loss of some current staff members who did not want to or could not relocate
4. The cost of the new site and equipment
5. The usual resistance factors to change
6. Jealousy of other staff members who want to move

Once again, after careful analysis, Marcie and the team concurred that the overall resistance to the proposed change was moderate to high, around 60. (See Figure 5-7).

Stage 3: Determine Whether to Implement the Change

If we plot the points on the graph, the results suggest that Marcie should take caution (quadrant A in Figure 5-8). As she proceeds with the change, she needs to move cautiously and try to reduce as many of the resisting factors as possible. If she does not, the change may not succeed. If the change fails, negativity increases. When the next change occurs, these same biochemists will be conditioned to be more resistant to it.

This method of analyzing whether to proceed with a change makes clear sense and is very proactive. It is not, however, a simple

Figure 5-7

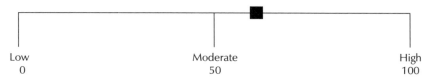

Level of Overall Resistance

process. Depending on the change being considered, many weeks of study are needed. But there is a big payoff for managers who do this analysis. When the change succeeds, staff will maintain a more positive attitude toward future changes. If done properly, the three-stage process will reduce negativity. Changes that would not succeed or have no reason for being implemented in the first place would not occur, thereby avoiding negative reactions to unnecessary change.

Figure 5-8

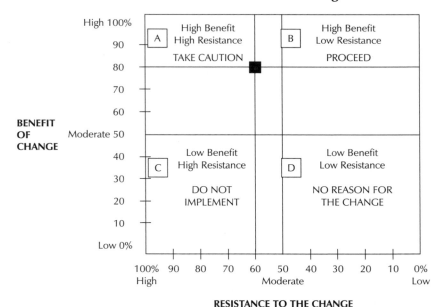

Proceed With Change?

THE CORRELATION BETWEEN RISK PERCEPTION, CHANGE, AND NEGATIVITY

Picture this scenario.

Three different companies, X, Y, and Z, are attempting to cross a busy freeway in order to get to the other side of town. Potentially, there is a big reward waiting for them there. However, it is a very risky undertaking to cross this busy freeway with cars going at rates of seventy and eighty miles an hour.

Company X looks to the right, then looks to the left, then looks to the right again, and so on, and never crosses.

Company Y looks to the right and thinks of all the benefits and resisting factors for crossing that way. Then it looks toward the left and does the same. Company Y has analyzed the best way to cross. It then crosses and goes to the other side of town.

During the time while Company X and Company Y were thinking about whether to cross or how to cross, Company Z already crossed. It was the first to get to the other side of town.

Think about and then answer this question. For which company (X, Y, or Z) would you like to work and why?

There is no right or best answer here. It is just that individuals have different perceptions of how change may be risky.

We would say that people who favor Company X are more risk-aversive. They like to take fewer risks and do not welcome change. They play it very safe.

Those who side with Company Y view change as intelligent risk-taking. They take the time to analyze the situation and then attempt to make the best possible decision.

Company Z people are big risk-takers. They move forward quickly and are willing to live with the consequences. In our scenario of crossing the busy freeway, Company Z crossed without a step-by-step plan. It took a big risk. It could have easily gotten hit by one of the speeding cars. The benefits of getting across the freeway would be high, though. It would have an edge on its competitors and be the first to the marketplace. In today's competitive business world, companies may have no other choice but to take big risks.

Here's the connection between risk, change, and negativity. A person who works in an environment that matches his or her comfort level of risk-taking will tend to be much more positive. If there is a mismatch between this person's perception of what a risky change situation is and the organization's reaction to risk or change, negativity becomes high.

Two things need to occur to reduce this potential mismatch that causes negativity. First, organizations need to be aware of the risk (change) perception of their staffs and take that into account when implementing change. Second, it is up to the individual to realize that he or she may not be working in the best possible environment for his or her personal risk-taking level.

SUMMARY

Change is a leading cause of workplace negativity. People become negative when the change is not implemented well by the organization or its leaders. People have different reactions to change and risk-taking. The individual must take some of the accountability for his or her reactions, but the larger responsibility lies with the organization and its managers. Managers also need to analyze a change before implementing it. Do the benefits of the change outweigh the resisting factors? Change in itself causes negativity. But when change does not succeed, negativity increases even more.

Chapter 6

The Imbalance between Trust and Enablement

We now examine the second major cause of negativity in organizations. We look at how the imbalance between trust and enablement causes negativity by using the trust matrix, with its "bunker people," "flying blind," and "caged eagles."

PROBLEMS WITH TRUST

A major cause of organizational negativity is the imbalance between trust and enablement. This imbalance problem may result in three staff conditions that cause organizational negativity: being entrenched in bunkers, flying blind, and being caged eagles.

Trust means allowing people to make decisions that affect their work. *Enablement* means giving individuals the skills, knowledge, resources, and motivation to do their jobs better. It means providing individuals with the opportunities for growth and development. When both trust and enablement are provided in the correct amount, or balanced, you get a positive work environment where loyalty tends to be high.

A mismatch between trust and enablement fosters negativity. People feel most positive about themselves and their workplaces when they are managed effectively. This balance between trust and enablement occurs when individuals are not oversupervised if they are highly skilled or undersupervised if they are new to the job or in a learning mode.

As shown in Figure 6-1, a manager or team leader can correct these three negative staff conditions by striking the right balance between trust and enablement (the lower right-hand quadrant, peak performers).

Let's look at the three imbalance conditions that are the culprits for negativity.

BEING ENTRENCHED IN BUNKERS

Organizations that do not enable or trust their employees retain individuals who are "entrenched in bunkers" (the upper left-hand quadrant of Figure 6-1). These individuals cannot or are not expected to do much, so they literally hide out. They try not to be seen, lay low, and keep out of harm's way.

Most people, on first impulse, would say that the entrenched-in-bunker group really wants to hide out and not do much. They might be correct about some of the bunker people, but this is definitely not true for most.

In general, depending on the company, about 80 percent of people who are entrenched in their bunkers really do not want to be (20 percent do not seem to mind). The

Figure 6-1

The Trust Matrix

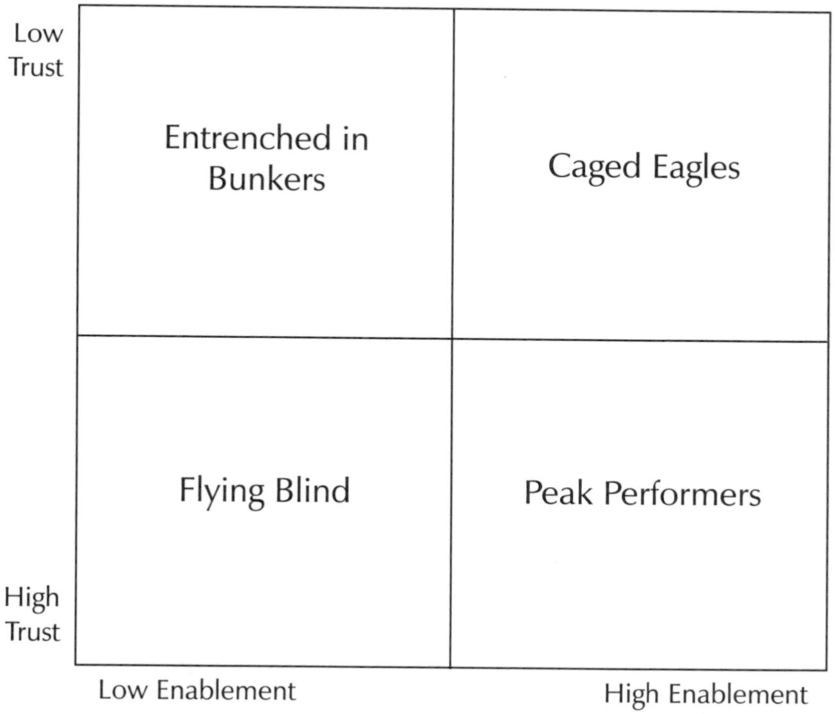

Low Trust	Entrenched in Bunkers	Caged Eagles
	Flying Blind	Peak Performers
High Trust	Low Enablement	High Enablement

organization or the manager, however, has made them hide out. Let me explain. People who do not have the skills or training to perform well, who are not given the opportunity to learn or develop themselves, or who have a poor job fit will entrench themselves for their own survival. The organization or manager even rewards them for staying in their bunkers by accepting that level of performance and giving raises and even promotions. You would think individuals would be happy with this scenario (they can just kick back and take it easy), but most lose their loyalty to organizations when organizations do not trust and enable them.

This entrenched condition causes high levels of negativity for two main reasons. First, the individual loses self-confidence in his or her abilities, and self-esteem suffers. This leads to negativity. Second, these people lose their pride in the organization. This also leads to negativity.

SCENARIO

Chi was hired as a programmer at a government agency in Washington, D.C., five years ago. This was his first job out of school, and he was planning on gaining some valuable experience before moving on to high-tech firms, his career goal. After about six months Chi realized that his rate of learning, as compared with that of his friends in other organizations, was not what he had anticipated. He was not exposed to the newest technology, and his management took very little interest in developing him or allowing him to make important decisions. They seemed, however, to be quite happy with his current work performance. Chi got the message early on that if he did exactly what he was told, made no decisions on his own, and caused no problems, he would do fine and even get raises and promotions.

Four and a half years later Chi is disillusioned and negative. He has lost his ability to move into the private sector because he realizes that his skills are not marketable in the corporate world. He has fallen greatly behind. But he is doing fairly well financially and has it pretty easy. There is no pressure on him at work, and he has an awful lot of days off. Nothing bad can happen to him if he keeps a low profile. He just goes about his business, keeping out of trouble, and spends most of his work time planning soccer workouts for the team he coaches.

The organization has not enabled Chi, and it has shown him little trust. It rewards him for doing mediocre work. Chi has become entrenched in his bunker. The imbalance with the entrenched-in-bunker people is their not having enough enablement and enough trust.

Solution

Organizations need to recruit people with the abilities or the potential abilities to succeed on the job. Then they have to train and develop them and provide them with excellent learning opportunities. Then they can trust them. For the 20 percent or so who are content being entrenched, accountability standards must be enforced.

THE FLYING BLIND

Companies that extend too much trust—blind trust—to employees but do not enable them create the "flying blind" (the lower left-hand quadrant of Figure 6-1). Here's how it happens. A department or an organization has work to do that individuals are not ready to handle. These individuals do not yet have the skills or expertise to perform at high levels, and the organization (or manager) leaves them alone, and they make big mistakes. And, to make matters worse, the flying blind get the blame. This causes the negativity.

SCENARIO

Deb Givens works for Abbot, Livingston, and Cartwright, a leading law firm in western Texas. Deb graduated near the top of her law class and did extremely well during the interview process at this firm. The partners believed that they had a winner on their hands. During the first few months of Deb's tenure, she was given cases that usually go to more senior attorneys. The partners had great confidence that she would be able to handle them. When Deb asked for some guidance, she was encouraged to work on her own and make her own decisions.

Deb was very concerned about her lack of experience, but, having the partners' command to move forward, she did. However, when she presented her briefs months later, these senior attorneys publicly chided her for her unprofessional work and immediately assigned her to more rote work.

Deb obviously needed coaching. She was not yet ready to handle these cases on her own. I am glad to say that Deb is now much more positive as she has found another law firm where she is getting what she needs.

Solution

To prevent the flying blind syndrome, organizations and managers need to guide their new or less experienced team members and monitor their performance closely. Once they see that these individuals can perform without high levels of maintenance, then they can give them more freedom to act on the job.

Some team members will never be able to perform well without closer supervision. These people may not have the abilities or motivation to do so. The organization then has two choices. It can keep monitoring these members to prevent them from becoming the flying blind. This takes a lot of work. Or it can find other positions for them, within or outside of the organization, where these individuals will be able to succeed.

CAGED EAGLES

In contrast to the flying blind, some companies have highly enabled people but do not trust them. They force people to become "caged eagles" (the upper right-hand quadrant of Figure 6-1), an especially negative scenario in today's marketplace.

Employees who are ready to learn and grow but do not get the opportunity to do so develop a negative view of their employer. They feel trapped and will do anything to get out. They often "jump ship" for another company. Meanwhile, the organization thinks that these peak performers left for more money. Companies often fail to see the real reason for their turnover: They have turned these staff members into caged eagles.

These performers are the ones sought after in today's marketplace. If they think and feel that they are being held back, they will literally leave or stop performing at high levels. When organizations talk about retention, these are the staff members they are usually talking about. In order to retain them, you must demonstrate high levels of trust. Those companies that perform at very high levels have few, if any, caged eagles.

Scenario

Pamela Teagardens is what anyone would call a peak performer. She has all the skills, knowledge, and experience to do her job as a senior consultant at an assisted living development firm in Western Europe. If that isn't enough, she is highly motivated and willing to do anything to ensure her own or the company's success.

Unfortunately, Pam is given very little freedom on the job. Her boss, Girt, has asked her to speak to him before she makes any decision or acts on her own. Basically, Girt wants it his way. He listens to Pam's input and suggestions but rarely acts on them. This is a new experience for Pam. In her previous jobs she was able to work on her own, without close supervision. Pam flourished in those environments. Here, working with Girt, she is wilting. When caged eagles cannot get out, they stop fighting to get out or die. Pam certainly won't die from being in this situation, but she will either stop doing well and become a performance problem or find herself another position.

Solution

When you are lucky enough to find an excellent and motivated performer or develop one of your existing staff members into one, do not cage them in. Give them the freedom (trust them) to work on their own and to make important decisions. They need to be constantly challenged and rewarded for their successes.

PEAK PERFORMERS

The goal of all organizations and their leaders and managers should be to get as many people as possible into the peak performer category (see the lower right-hand quadrant in Figure 6-2). The message is obvious for those who

Figure 6-2

The Trust Matrix

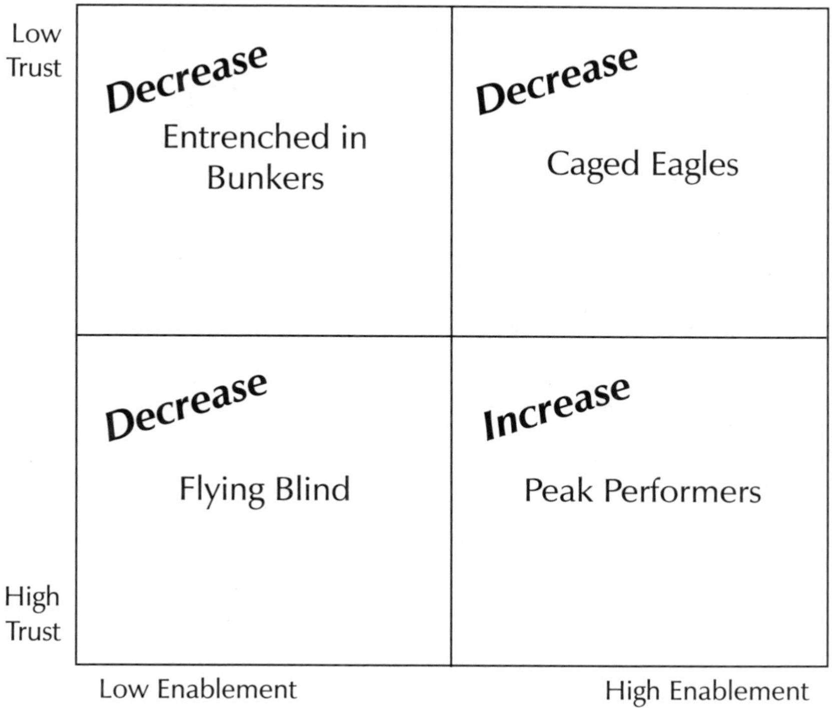

	Low Enablement	High Enablement
Low Trust	**Decrease** Entrenched in Bunkers	**Decrease** Caged Eagles
High Trust	**Decrease** Flying Blind	**Increase** Peak Performers

want to reduce organizational negativity: Reduce the number of people who are entrenched in bunkers, are flying blind, or are caged eagles. Increase the numbers who are fully trusted.

According to the Malcolm Baldrige Service Award-Winning Companies, the best companies have more than 80 percent of their staff in the peak performers quadrant and 20 percent scattered through the other three quadrants. How would you distribute the percentages for your own department or organization?

SUMMARY

In Chapter 6 we saw that another major way to prevent departmental and organizational negativity is to find the right balance between enablement and trust. When organizations do not enable or trust their people, the condition known as "entrenched in bunkers" occurs. Here people cannot perform well and are not encouraged to do so. This leads to high levels of negativity. The condition of "flying blind" occurs when people are not enabled, but the organization gives them lots of trust anyway. These individuals usually fail and become negative because they are not ready to handle the job. Then there are the "caged eagles" who are enabled but not trusted. This frustrating situation causes them to become negative. An organization that both enables and trusts its employees is certain to develop a positive working environment and greatly reduce negativity.

Chapter 7

CHANGING THE ORGANIZATION'S NORMS AND CULTURE

Norms represent the expected and accepted behavior of individuals in departments, groups, teams, and the organization. Companies develop norms for just about everything one does at work: how to treat customers, delegate work, interact with others socially, take risks, and so forth. Ultimately, these norms shape an organization's personality or culture because they consist of the repeated behaviors of the majority.

Norms are

Never set in stone.

It may be difficult to do it, but they can always change.

Open expressions of what is valued.

That is why people do them.

Repeated behaviors.

The more they are done, the more they become accepted.

Majority behaviors.
    Most people do them, which influences others to do
    them as well.

    And as a result of these four, norms

Shape the personality or attitude of the organization.

    Sometimes norms result in behaviors and actions that
keep staff positive and benefit the organization. A New
York brokerage firm, for example, has established a strong
norm that meetings must start and end on time. Employees
speak highly of this norm because their time is valuable
and expensive, and they do not like to waste it.
    At the other end of the spectrum, norms can result in
negative behaviors and actions. A television production
company in Los Angeles has cross-functional multilevel
project teams to decide what new properties to produce.
But the top-level "team" members, the directors, dominate
the discussions and decisions. Lower-level members never
get a chance to voice their opinions. The company says
these teams are learning opportunities for less experienced
staff members, but this norm on decision-making causes
employees to become negative about their value to the
company. A staff member below the director level may
have a better idea or approach for a new project, but no
one will ever know—not at this studio, at least.
    The good news is that norms can be changed. In this
chapter we look at the four steps you can take to turn a
negative culture into a positive one. The more negative
norms you turn into positive norms, the less negative your
work environment will be.

THE FOUR-STEP PROCESS FOR CHANGING NORMS

Here are the four steps:

Step 1

Conduct a cultural audit: Describe the current organizational, department, or group norms.

Step 2

Describe what you want the new organizational, department, or group norms (culture) to be. That is, what new norms will replace the old ones?

Step 3

Describe exactly how you will change from the current norms to the new norms. An action plan is needed for each norm change.

Step 4

Implement the action plans and follow up to make sure the new norms are being adhered to. Reward those individuals who have changed to the new norms and hold those who have not accountable.

What we are really talking about in this four-step process is changing inappropriate or negative norms into appropriate or positive norms. When you do this, you change the negative culture of an organization to a positive one.

An organization's culture is made up of seven interdependent norm categories:

1. Organizational pride
2. Teamwork
3. Communication
4. Rewarded behaviors
5. Accountability
6. Decision-making power
7. Supervision

You change culture by changing the norms within each of these seven categories. The more norms you change, the more the culture changes. The more negative norms you change into positive ones, the more the culture changes from a negative one into a positive one. Let's describe what is meant by each of these categories.

1. ORGANIZATIONAL PRIDE

You are listening in on conversations held in company cafeterias, employee lounges, before and after meetings, and in the parking lots. What is the staff saying about the company? Are they saying positive things, such as "This is the best place I have ever worked" or "Managers really help us out around here" or "We are definitely serving the needs of the community"? Or are they saying negative things, such as "What a boring place! Nothing exciting happens around here" or "I cannot believe they promoted her!" or "I wish they would tell us what was going on"?

Organizational pride is defined as what people say about the company that they work for—what they tell their friends, relatives, and acquaintances. If I were to meet people from your company at a social gathering, on a plane, or in a queue, and we were sharing what it is like to work at our respective companies, how would they be describing their work environments? What are their opinions of the services or products their organization provides?

2. TEAMWORK

We are not talking about whether your firm is team-based. What is meant here is how people work together. Are there high levels of cooperation? Do departments compete against one another or help out one another? Do team members share information with one another or protect it to gain power? Is everyone in the organization working toward meeting the same customer goals? Do different levels work together, or is there a strong hierarchy system that does not make everyone feel like he or she is part of the team?

3. COMMUNICATION

Communication is defined as how information is disseminated. Some questions to ask that determine the communication culture in your organization include the following:

- What types of conflicts are there, and how are they managed?
- Is communication one-way or two-way? Is it downward only, or is input allowed from those below?

- How are meetings run? Are they effective?
- Is the organization's technology for communicating state-of-the-art?
- Are people informed? Do they know what is going on?
- How are changes communicated?

4. REWARDED BEHAVIORS

This fourth criterion that determines organizational culture is not what type of reward people receive for good performance or behavior, such as bonuses, promotions, plaques, and so on. It is the types of behaviors or actions that people get rewarded for. For example, is risk-taking, speaking up, or expressing different opinions from the established ones rewarded or punished? Are mistakes allowed or forbidden?

Also within this category of rewarded behaviors are people's personal characteristics. Individuals often get rewarded (or punished) for having certain characteristics. These characteristics include ethnicity, gender, educational level, marital status, age, personal appearance, social status, and hobbies and interests.

5. ACCOUNTABILITY

If individuals, teams, or departments do not meet standards, expectations, goals, and so on, how are they held accountable? Is there any accountability, or can people do whatever they wish? If one does not complete projects on time, has excessive errors, or does not show up for work on a regular basis, what can be done? Are accountability standards reasonable, severe, or too lenient? Are certain people held accountable and not others?

6. Decision-Making Power

This next category of defining culture means how involved the individual is in making decisions about the work that affects him or her. Do people have any say in changing work procedures, redesigning the products, providing the services, coming up with different ways of doing things? Which of the five following levels of decision-making is characteristic of your culture?

- All decisions are made from the top, with no input from the staff.
- All decisions are made from the top, with some input from the staff.
- There is joint decision-making.
- Staff makes decisions that affect their work, with the approval of the top.
- Staff makes all decisions. Top management relies on the staff for their decision-making ability.

7. Supervision

Think of the best supervisor you have ever worked for, currently work for, or could imagine working for. What about this person makes him or her so effective? Your answer to this question will allow you to compare your description of the "ideal" supervisor to the current state of supervision within your team, department, or organization.

Case Study: Cerro Medical Center

Cerro Medical Center is located in the suburbs of New York City. It is one of the area's largest medical centers, has been in operation for more than thirty years, and employs 1,500 people. The new hospital administrator, Jim Rivera, analyzed the impact that negativity was having on the Medical Center and decided to make an all-out effort to change Cerro's negative work culture into a positive one.

One of Cerro's most negative departments was human resources (HR). High turnover, lower production levels, and customer complaints (both from internal customers and patients and their families) were the driving forces for Jim's desire to change the culture of HR. Jim had decided that HR was going to be his prototype in this cultural change process. He hoped to take this "transformation" success and do the same for many other departments in the center.

Step 1. Conduct a Cultural Audit

Jim's first step was to do a cultural audit in which he described the HR Department's norms (culture). He and members of a change team (both hospital staff and outside consultants) that he formed conducted interviews and distributed surveys and questionnaires to determine the current norms. Here were the findings of the change team:

1. Department/Organizational Pride

Staff basically bad-mouthed the department. They did not like working there. They did not like their remote location, their department head, or the way decisions were made. Their view of the HR Department contaminated their pride in working at the center. When asked what would be the best change that could happen, most responded, "Finding a new job at a different medical center."

2. Teamwork

The HR Department was divided into four units: wage and salary, employment, employee training and development, and labor relations. Each had a supervisor. Most staff believed there was little cooperation among the units. They believed, in fact, that the units were vying for funds and the attention of the manager, Janice Stile. It was very rare for members of one unit to socialize with the members of the others.

3. Communication

Staff felt that communication was good within their own units but nonexistent among the four units. Supervisors only communicated directly with Janice, never with one another. There was a strict top-down communication structure to the department. If a staff member from labor relations, for example, wanted to send some information to a staff member from wage and salary, he or she would have to go through their respective supervisors first. Both staff and supervisors believed that they knew very little of what the center's other units or other departments were doing.

4. Rewarded Behaviors

All staff within the department, including Janice, stated that rewarded behaviors were the ones that their boss expected them to do. As long as they did what they were told, things were fine. Good attendance and punctuality, always being able to be located, no telecommuting, writing excellent memos, and keeping neat offices were very admirable traits. Voicing one's opinion or disagreeing with top management philosophy would get you into a lot of trouble. However, complaining about the physical work space and the lack of sophisticated computerization systems would put you in good standing.

5. Accountability

This varied depending on level. Most staff said there was a high level of accountability and that their work was monitored very closely. They believed, however, that their supervisors always blamed them for their own mistakes. On the other hand, supervisors and Janice said that their employees needed to be held more accountable but that the center's rules and regulations protected the employees too much.

6. Decision-Making Power

Here there was universal agreement. No one, not even Janice, thought that he or she had a say in important decisions affecting his or her work. Everyone mentioned that decisions came from top management.

7. Supervision

Staff acknowledged that upper management tied their supervisors' and Janice's hands. Still, however, they expected their immediate boss to be more understanding and responsive to their needs. They rarely felt motivated at work. They noted that their supervisors and Janet had the knowledge and technical skills to do well but lacked the people skills so crucial to managing.

Step 2. Describe What You Want the New HR Department Norms (Culture) to Be

As a result of conducting the attitude audit, Jim Rivera and the change team were able to identify the major factors contributing to the negative culture of the HR Department. Their next step was to decide what new norms they wanted to take the place of the current ones. By combining the recommendations of the HR staff with their own views, Jim and the change team came up with a new set of norms that would be the department's goal. Briefly, this was their vision of the "new" HR Department.

1. Department/Organizational Pride

Staff would speak up about how the HR Department was contributing to the success of the Medical Center. They would say that they enjoyed working there and appreciate the contributions that all staff members were making. The goal was to have staff truly believe this and do it voluntarily.

2. Teamwork

The change would be to have the entire staff feel like they were one team and that they needed to be interdependent to achieve their goals. Regardless of level or what unit they worked in, everyone would cooperate with one another.

3. Communication

Communication would be two-way, whereby staff felt comfortable communicating upwardly and supervisors and Janice would encourage such behavior. Communication between and among units would increase, and the staff would feel free to talk with anyone in the HR Department. Janice would share all information that would facilitate the staff's performing their jobs better and educate them about what was happening in the Medical Center.

4. Rewarded Behaviors

The shift here would be to having the staff share their differing opinions and respect them for so doing. Supervisors and Janice would incorporate their ideas and encourage "thinking outside of the box." Talking up the department and the center would be encouraged. Staff would be motivated to find their own ways of getting the work done; they would not just follow orders from the bosses.

5. Accountability

Goals and objectives for each team member would be established in partnership with their immediate boss, and their success would be measured against the achievement of these goals. These goals would be aligned with those of the HR Department. Each staff member would be held accountable for meeting his or her own goals.

6. Decision-Making Power

Staff members at all levels would become actively involved in making decisions that affect their work and the mission of the HR Department. The purpose of meetings would now be to make decisions, with all parties involved, not just to disseminate information.

7. Supervision

Supervisors and Janice would build stronger relationships with each member of their staff. They would need to listen to them more, be supportive, constantly provide feedback, and motivate them to perform at their highest levels.

Step 3. Describe Exactly How You Will Change from the Current Norms to the New Norms

Step 3, in which an action plan is devised for each norm change, is the pivotal step in changing inappropriate norms. Teams, departments, or organizations can usually complete the first two steps successfully, even though they are challenging. Organizations are able to recognize what is not working or what is causing negativity and what they would like to see in its place to build a positive work environment. It is Step 3, however, that many organizations find quite difficult to do. This is because it is very hard work. The organization has to identify in very specific terms exactly how it will change its negative norms from Step 1 into the positive norms from Step 2. I strongly believe that many more work environments would be much less negative if organizations took the time and energy needed to complete Step 3. It is rare, unfortunately, for a negative workplace to go beyond Step 2. That is why so few of them ever turn into positive environments.

1. Department/Organizational Pride

CURRENT NORM

The staff (all levels) speaks poorly of their remote location.

NEW NORM

Have the staff speak in positive terms about their location.

POSSIBLE ACTION PLANNING STEPS

- Relocate HR Department to the main building of the Medical Center.
- Have senior management visit the current site more often.
- Guarantee that the site receives all of the same information at the same time as the rest of the center.

- Improve the physical working conditions of the remote site.
- Move another critical function to the site, such as one of the senior manager positions, to give it more credibility.

2. Teamwork

CURRENT NORM

Units do not cooperate with one another.

NEW NORM

There is open, active cooperation between and among units.

POSSIBLE ACTION PLANNING STEPS

- The department head emphasizes the importance of team-work and cooperation.
- Team-building sessions are held to establish a one-department philosophy.
- Performance evaluations are changed to reflect cooperation among team members.
- Bonuses or salary increases are partially contingent on the success of all of the units.
- All units are encouraged to attend the celebrations, parties, and events of any one unit.

3. Communication

CURRENT NORM

Communication from Janice to supervisors and supervisors to the unit staff is one-way: top down.

NEW NORM

Two-way communication is encouraged and expected.

POSSIBLE ACTION PLANNING STEPS

- Supervisors and Janice hold meetings to describe this new approach.

- Staff members' and supervisors' ideas and opinions are used and rewarded.
- Supervisors and Janice facilitate a two-way dialogue and make it part of their everyday behaviors.

4. Rewarded Behaviors

CURRENT NORM

Risk-taking is discouraged.

NEW NORM

Risk-taking is encouraged.

POSSIBLE ACTION PLANNING STEPS

- Individuals are not punished for making mistakes.
- Creative or new solutions to existing problems are rewarded.
- Training sessions on how to take intelligent risks are held.
- Innovative strategies are publicly acknowledged. They are published in the center's newsletter; senior managers are informed of who came up with the new approach; or notices are posted around the center.

5. Accountability

CURRENT NORM

Staff believes they are held accountable; the supervisors and Janice believe that they are not.

NEW NORM

There is agreement on what it means to be accountable, accountability measures are developed, and staff is held accountable.

POSSIBLE ACTION PLANNING STEPS

- Accountability standards for each position are developed with agreement from staff.

- A third party reviews the accountability standards and confirms their applicability or suggests new standards.
- Once the accountability standards are accepted, staff is expected to meet them.
- Supervisors and Janice are given training on how to measure the achievement of accountability standards and how to communicate to their staff members the accomplishment or nonaccomplishment of these standards.

6. Decision-Making Power

CURRENT NORM

The manager makes the decision and then informs the staff of what they have to do.

NEW NORM

Before a decision is made, the staff are asked for their views or opinions.

POSSIBLE ACTION PLANNING STEPS

- Inform and educate Janice as to why this change is important.
- Inform and educate the staff to enable them to participate in decision-making.
- As part of the company management-training program, Janice is taught how to involve others in decision-making.

7. Supervision

CURRENT NORM

Supervisors do not give regular feedback to their staff.

NEW NORM

Supervisors need to give continual feedback to their staff on how they are performing.

POSSIBLE ACTION PLANNING STEPS

- Supervisors hold weekly sessions to discuss work performance with their staff.
- Janice monitors the behaviors of supervisors to assure that this occurs.
- Supervisors are educated about the significance of continual feedback and how to deliver it.
- Staff receives training on how to receive feedback without becoming defensive.

As you can see, Step 3 could be a long, detailed, and time-consuming process. One must have the commitment of all parties involved. As previously mentioned, many organizations do not bother with Step 3 and wonder why the norms have not changed. These organizations will never succeed in eliminating negativity unless they take the time and effort to complete this step. Then they will be able to proceed with Step 4.

Step 4. Implementation and Follow-up

Implement the action plans from Step 3 and follow up to make sure that the new norms are being adhered to. Reward those individuals who have changed to the new norms and hold those who have not accountable.

Step 4 also tends to get ignored by organizations. The new appropriate norms never shape the personality of the organization unless Step 4 happens.

Jim had to take big steps if he expected the HR Department staff to accept the new norms. He had to make some big changes to the performance review process as well as job descriptions and responsibilities if he expected these new norms to stick.

Let's look at three of the change examples from Step 3 to see how Jim Rivera followed up and either rewarded or held HR staff accountable.

Teamwork

NEW NORM

There is open, active cooperation between and among departments.

Jim changed the center's performance review from one of recognizing individual contribution to also recognizing team contribution. HR staff soon got the message that it "paid" to be a team player. Their teamwork got them better performance ratings and opportunities for promotion. The reverse occurred if they did not become team players. If they did not conform to the new, desired team behaviors, they got lower ratings, had no opportunity for advancement, and eventually were terminated.

Rewarded Behaviors

NEW NORM

Risk-taking is encouraged.

When staff took the intelligent risks they were encouraged to, letters went into their performance files, upper management called to thank them, and they received cash bonuses.

Also, as part of this new norm, staff had to demonstrate throughout the year that they were taking risks. It was now considered a requirement of the job. If they didn't, their jobs were in jeopardy.

Supervision

NEW NORM

Supervisors need to give continual feedback to staff on how the staff is performing.

The supervisors' and Janice's job descriptions were changed to include the requirement that they give informal feedback to each staff member at least four times a year. Their performance evaluations and salary increases were tied to doing this. If they did not give feedback on a regular basis, their supervisory positions became tenuous. Additionally, Jim was now having employees rate their supervisors. This was another powerful way of showing supervisors and Janice that they were being held accountable for doing what they were supposed to.

SUMMARY

In Chapter 7 we reviewed how to change norms, which in turn changes culture. We saw that it is not an easy process but one that must take place if negativity is to be eliminated. Remember that completing only the first two steps in the change process is not enough. Success will only come by completing Steps 3 and 4 as well.

Norms have really changed at Cerro's HR Department. Team spirit and teamwork are the new norms, as are two-way communication, involvement in decision-making, effective supervision, and accountability. Now that Jim Rivera and the change team have put into practice the four-step process for changing negative or inappropriate norms into positive or appropriate ones, they will begin working on many other departments within the Medical Center.

Chapter 8

OTHER STRATEGIES TO ELIMINATE ORGANIZATIONAL NEGATIVITY

In this chapter I address a few other strategies for combating organizational, departmental, and group negativity:

1. Developing a learning environment
2. Meeting the staff's motivational needs
3. Encouraging creativity
4. Hiring a "jollyologist"

1. DEVELOPING A LEARNING ENVIRONMENT

As discussed in Chapter 6, companies that balance enablement and trust have the most positive work environments. Building what is called a learning environment is another way to enable and then to trust people. It is very rare to find a learning environment and negativity at the same time. Also, most of today's employees will expect to have a learning environment. If they do not find one, they will become negative.

A learning environment occurs under these conditions:

- The organization supports, recognizes, and rewards people for learning.
- Employees become integral to the decision-making process, making them part of the "brain" of the organization.

To determine if yours is a learning environment, ask yourself these questions:

- Is there a general attitude in my department or organization that people are to always try to better themselves through continuous learning?
- Are individual, team, and departmental goals set as a means of establishing learning plans?
- Does my department or organization have incentive rewards to motivate employees for developing new skills?
- Does my department or organization value innovation and experimentation?
- Is there an environment of open communication?
- Does my organization actively seek feedback from those closest to the service or the product?
- Does my department or organization know the trends in its field; does it stay current on the latest technological changes?
- Do managers believe in developing their staffs?

The more affirmative responses you have to these questions, the more likely that your work environment is a positive one that encourages learning. If you have more than two or three negative responses, you are inviting negativity in.

As Figure 8-1 shows, organizations and their managers not only need to provide people with the skills and competencies to succeed now, but also to prepare them to meet the organization's future needs.

A learning environment enables people. When people are enabled, they feel much less negative. They feel trusted. They also trust that the organization is interested in them.

2. MEETING THE STAFF'S MOTIVATIONAL NEEDS

Positive workplaces have motivated staff members. These organizations make sure that the motivational needs of

Figure 8-1

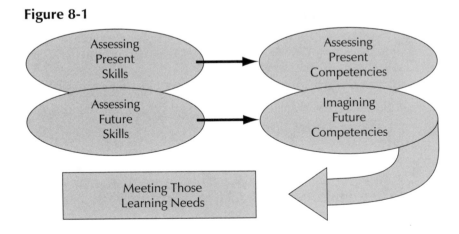

staff are met and satisfied. The company must provide good working conditions and competitive salary and benefits packages. They must also reward staff for excellent performance through their bonus and profit-sharing plans. However, managers and leaders have the big responsibility of motivating others. They have to make sure that their staffs stay motivated over long periods of time. Managers and leaders have the following motivational needs to satisfy:

1. The Achievement Need

- Ensure that goals are set and monitored on an ongoing basis.
- If goals are in jeopardy, discuss them and provide support and suggestions to ensure that they are met.

2. The Responsibility Need

- Provide opportunities for employees to be influential.
- Provide opportunities for employees to organize and direct an activity.

3. The Recognition Need

- Provide opportunities for the worker to be visible.
- Establish a relationship that provides positive feedback and attention.

4. The Interesting Work Need

- Give employees a chance to take on a new responsibility as a part of their duties.

- Be open to innovative ideas and different ways of doing the work.

5. The Growth Need

- Offer training opportunities—in-house or from an outside source.
- Offer your employee the opportunity to team up with someone else to learn a new skill.

6. The Empowerment Need

- Let staff make decisions that affect their work.
- Let them work on their own without direct supervision.

Organizations and their managers must also be aware of what *not* to do if they seek to improve motivation. Please avoid these two pitfalls. They are the two biggest causes of loss of motivation in organizations.

- Managers and organizations punish their excellent performers. They give them more work to do, usually more of the same. They do not let them go off to conferences and conventions. After all, who is going to do the work around the office? I have even known managers who will not promote their best. They do not want to lose them. Eventually these performers will get the message that it does not pay to be so good around here. Eventually, their work quality declines, and their negativity increases.
- Managers and organizations reward their poorer performers. They give them less work to do, easier assign-

ments, or better projects. They continue to give them raises and bonuses. Then there are those managers who will promote a person out of their group just to get rid of him or her. These employees may be feeling happy, but all the others become very negative.

A manager at a disk drive manufacturing company once had a very difficult employee who should have been fired, but she did not want to take the time and effort to do it. So she "enhanced" his record and put it in the Intranet system, and in the course of a few days some other department took him. It was a promotion. And this is what everyone has been doing with this employee for the past five years. He is now a vice president! (That could be why this company is in so much trouble today.) The irony of the story is that as a result of the last reorganization, the manager now reports to the guy she couldn't be bothered to fire. Divine justice, I say.

The message is clear. Do not punish your excellent performers. Do not reward your poorer performers.

3. ENCOURAGING CREATIVITY

A manager must be sensitive to the creative needs of his or her employee population and design ways to meet these needs while still achieving the organization's goals. (In fact, creative employees are usually important contributors to reaching those goals.) Organizations that encourage a creative atmosphere have a much more positive culture. It is very rare to find negativity in an organization that promotes creative thinking and innovation.

To encourage a creative workplace, organizations and their managers need to do the following:

- Present problem situations as challenging opportunities.
- Make sure employees realize that creative ideas are wanted and expected from everyone.
- Invite creative participation from all those who will be affected by a decision.
- Tolerate failure as an expected part of creativity; make it safe to take risks.
- Recognize and reward a creative contribution.
- Provide everyone with training in the basics of creativity.
- Get to know employees as individuals to learn their creativity needs.

4. HIRE A "JOLLYOLOGIST"

A "jollyologist" (a Ph.D. in positive behavior and morale boosting) has the responsibility of bringing fun to the workplace and eliminating negativity. I have seen jollyologists have much success in several companies.

Here are just several of the interventions that jollyologists I have known have introduced in their companies:

- Staff laughs. The jollyologist gathers the staff together, tells a funny story about a customer or client, and waits for everyone to laugh.

▪ Bring your pet to work week. Staff are allowed to bring their pets to work as long as the pets behave. People become much more positive and calm. Productivity always seems to rise, and negative conflicts disappear during this week. Companies such as Audodesk allow pets every day of the year.

▪ Jeopardy. The staff plays the game at lunch, and all the questions in response to answers have to be about the company and have to be funny.

▪ Going Hollywood. Staff members dress up and act like their movie star look-alikes for one day.

▪ The office is decorated with balloons and streamers for no specific reason.

▪ Sirens go off whenever negativity is expressed.

▪ Spotlights are beamed on people with negative expressions.

▪ Brainstorming sessions are held on how to improve team spirit.

▪ The jollyologist decides who are the most spirited and positive employees each month. They get reserved parking or valet service.

▪ Medical day. All the staff get surgical masks, positive pills (sugar-coated), and "negativity" flu shots that immunize them from workplace negativity.

SUMMARY

In addition to our three major interventions to eliminate workplace negativity—managing change, correcting the imbalance between trust and enablement, and changing norms—there are a few other ways to also eliminate negativity in organizations. The learning environment gets people to trust and become loyal to their company; meeting motivational needs allows people to perform at their best; encouraging creativity ensures a positive approach to work; and hiring a jollyologist (or using your own employee volunteers) guarantees a fun, upbeat environment.

Chapter 9

THE THREE POWERS OF A POSITIVE ATTITUDE

Let's revisit Strategy 24, the AAA approach discussed in Chapter 2. People exposed to negativity on a daily basis at their workplaces have three choices. They can try to avoid the negativity (that may be impossible), they can try to change it (what most of this book is about), or they just may have to learn to accept it. That is, they may have little ability to change the work environment, hold people accountable, or use many of the techniques or strategies I have discussed. If that is your situation or that of your colleagues, you must protect yourself and them with the three powers of a positive attitude. These powers will guarantee that you or anyone else using them or exposed to them has immunity against workplace negativity.

THE THREE POWERS OF A POSITIVE ATTITUDE

The three powers of a positive attitude lead to a positive work environment. It is nearly impossible for negativity to survive against them. Ask yourself this question: "How can I give myself, or teach others, these three powers?"

1. A positive, fun attitude that causes good things to happen
   Do you or your colleagues have this power?
2. A creative attitude that sees new ideas and many other solutions
   Do you or your colleagues have this power?
3. An energizing attitude that triggers enthusiasm
   Do you or your colleagues have this power?

Let's look at each one in greater detail and see how people have developed these powers.

A Positive, Fun Attitude That Causes Good Things to Happen

People with this power enjoy life and like what they are doing. They communicate this attitude to all those around them. Often their attitude is contagious. They find positive things to say about their jobs, the people with whom they work, the services or products the organization provides, the customers, the boss, and so on. They try to make work fun; they laugh a lot, smile, joke around somewhat, and are playful. They also make those around them feel motivated, important, and productive.

Case Study: Jesse Black

Jesse used to go to work wishing he wasn't there and counting the hours on the clock. He disliked everyone around him. He considered his peers intellectual inferiors and his boss no more than a necessary evil he had to deal with. He would also get down on himself for being stuck in his job and not making more of his life.

Jesse was not all that different outside the office. Most of the time he would complain about things and belittle the efforts of his wife and children. He disliked where he lived and begrudgingly spoke to his neighbors.

About five years ago, Jesse had this incredible flash while riding Metro North into Grand Central Station in New York City. The train suddenly stopped and the lights went out. The conductor said, "We are stuck in the tunnel indefinitely. There will be no more announcements until we start moving again." Jesse's true behaviors came out during that wait. He lashed out at Metro North, his fellow passengers, his lousy job that forced him to commute two hours a day, and other aspects of his life. Jesse couldn't believe how he sounded. Then he calmed down and listened to the other passengers. They were much more optimistic and started to joke around and laugh. Jesse thought to himself, "How come I cannot do this? It seems like a much better way to be."

He finally admitted to himself that he was negative and a bore to all around him. Behaving in this manner was of no help to him or to anyone else he encountered. From that moment on, Jesse decided he was going to come across differently. He was going to be fun and positive to be around. At least he would see if the kind of reaction he got from others would be different.

It has not been an easy transformation for Jesse. For years, he was much more comfortable being the pessimist. But with solid determination and hard work, Jesse's fun and positive attitude won out. He practiced saying positive things, gave others deserved compliments, enjoyed himself more, and made light of unavoidable stressful situations.

Jesse has the same job and boss, the same wife and children, and the same neighbors. And he still commutes each day. But his attitude has changed. He now communicates in an upbeat, positive mood; he is fun to be around and repels negativity. His positive, fun attitude gets a much better reaction from people. He is a catalyst for good things to happen. He also likes himself much more. Jesse definitely has acquired the first power of a positive attitude.

A Creative Attitude That Sees New Ideas and Many Other Solutions

People and organizations with this power are focused on how they can make things better at work. They do not complain or moan but look for better answers. They believe it best to create solutions for the challenges facing them. They are willing to do things a different way, are open to all possibilities, and find it fun and enjoyable to be creative.

Case Study: DAZ

In the Sales and Marketing Department at DAZ, one of the country's largest manufacturers of automobile supplies, a creative attitude is required. Staff is constantly challenged to come up with new procedures, recommendations, and new markets. As soon as you walk into the facility you are inundated with the message that new ideas are the norm. There are suggestion boxes strategically located, managers are required to hold two twenty-minute revenue-increasing brainstorming sessions a day, the company library is filled with books and exercises on creativity, and every employee must attend a creativity workshop every three months. The employee of the month receives a cash bonus of $1,000. The employee gets this reward because he or she was able to come up with a creative solution that made or saved the company a lot of money.

At DAZ, the status quo is not acceptable. If a staff member cannot offer new thoughts, opinions, or ideas, he or she is not needed. A large part of one's employee evaluation is based on one's creativity quotient. And we are talking about everyone in this department of fifty. Creativity is the firm's driving force. As a result of this creativity effort, profits at DAZ have skyrocketed, and market share has increased.

Negativity is nonexistent. There is no time or tolerance for it. People are always thinking of better ways of doing things, not complaining about the way things are. As part of the interview process, each prospective employee is asked to define what he or she believes is meant by the three powers of a positive attitude and then to give real-life examples of how he or she has used these powers. Listening in on one of these interviews is quite a powerful experience.

The Sales and Marketing Department at DAZ definitely has the second power of a positive attitude.

AN ENERGIZING ATTITUDE THAT TRIGGERS ENTHUSIASM

Those with this power are able to make colleagues and staff more productive. They build up others' self-esteem, get them excited about what they are doing, and show them how their work affects the rest of the organization. They have a bottom-line quality drive that gets communicated to others. When you work with someone with this power, you cannot wait to get to work.

CASE STUDY: BELINDA ROSS

Belinda Ross is a supervisor in the Document Department of the Bureau of Child Support and Enforcement in New York City. The bureau is responsible for getting absent parents to pay for the support of their children once the Courts have required them to do so. Morale is generally low and negativity high at the bureau. First, the nature of the business leads to many difficult encounters with these absent parents. Second, the bureau is a bureaucracy. Decision-making is top-down, and promotional opportunities are based on seniority, not capability. Pay is adequate but not great. A great performer does not receive any more money than a mediocre or poor one. Finally, the working conditions are not great. The furniture is old, the equipment is outdated, the air-conditioning and heat are unreliable, and the elevators are a crapshoot.

However, when we come to Belinda Ross's unit, things are different. Physically it looks like every other unit in the building, but something is happening there that you cannot find anywhere else. What is happening is the third power of a positive attitude: Belinda has the energizing attitude, and she triggers good things wherever she goes.

Belinda always shows up on time, works hard, and encourages her staff to do so as well. She always reminds them of their mission of collecting monies for the support of children. She never negatively criticizes her job, her colleagues, or the work environment. She is always constructive. She smiles appropriately, is cheerful and motivating, always uses positive statements, and speaks in an assertive tone. She accepts the bureau for what it is and realizes that change will take many years and is pretty much out of her control. Her energy seems to spread like a tidal wave throughout her unit and really to anyone that she comes into contact with. She has the lowest turnover rate of the entire agency, and her staff consistently gets rated in the top performance categories on their 360-degree feedback reports.

When I asked Belinda what drives her to be so enthusiastic, she replied, "What's the alternative? I could sit around like others and bemoan my fate or become negative and waste a lot of energy. Or I could put my energy to productive use. Which do you think makes me and the people around me happier?"

Belinda definitely has the third power.

These three powers are not elusive: They are demonstrated every day in all different kinds of places. Practitioners of these powers seem to block out the negativity around them, and, equally important, they positively influence the attitudes of others.

To test yourself on the three powers, see if you can answer affirmatively to all of the following questions:

1. Can you just show up for work and have fun if you decided to?
2. Could you develop an original competitive game

that two or more people could play just using the materials from the top of your desk?

3. Are you always trying to think of different and better ways to do things?
4. Do your colleagues smile when they see you?
5. Can you motivate others to achieve their goals and dreams?
6. Do you not allow mistakes or failures to erode your self-image?
7. Are you unafraid to be measured against others' expectations?
8. Do you use positive words or expectations in conversation?
9. Do you believe that you have the knowledge, abilities, intuition, and know-how to handle a challenging task?
10. Do you stay committed to finishing what you have started?
11. Do you have a high level of interest, positive energy, passion, and personal motivation?
12. Do you trust in yourself and others to provide support and guidance when needed?
13. Are you willing to take risks and overcome fears even when the outcome is uncertain?
14. Do you find ways of making the seemingly impossible possible?
15. Do you choose the "kernel" of good ideas and expand on them?
16. Do you listen, understand, and discuss?
17. Do you allow time for others to express themselves?

18. Are you considerate of others and their points of view, and do you avoid using inappropriate facial expressions?
19. Do you want to find the best solution rather than always needing to be "right"?
20. Do you see obstacles as challenges to meet and overcome?

If you answered affirmatively to almost all of these questions, it will be almost impossible for you to become negative or become affected by a negative work environment. It is also highly likely that your workplace will be a very positive one.

When these three major attacks on the virus succeed, organizations create a positive workplace. The negativity virus has been cured.

Appendix A

A NEGATIVITY ASSESSMENT

Before reading this section, take the following assessment to determine how negative a place yours really is. You may be surprised!

The assessment is divided into three sections. Answer yes or no to each item. The more yes responses you have, the more positive your workplace is. The more no responses you have, the more you need to focus on how to address the negativity. You can also determine where more effort is needed—organization, department, or team negativity.

NEGATIVITY ASSESSMENT QUESTIONNAIRE

Pertaining to the Organization

1. Is this organization doing well, and will it continue to do well?
2. Do people enjoy and feel secure in their jobs?
3. Does top management have a clear sense of how

to make the organization successful, and are they considered competent?

4. Are people proud of their organization?
5. Given other job opportunities, would most employees choose to stay here?

Pertaining to the Department

6. Is your department generally considered a good place to work in the organization?
7. Do other groups consider your department to be a competent component in the organization?
8. Is morale high?
9. Is the manager of your department considered highly competent and a good leader?

Pertaining to Your Team/Group

10. Do they rarely complain or gripe?
11. Does your team leader give your group a strong sense of where it is going and what it needs to do to get there?
12. Does your team go the extra mile?
13. Does your team leader provide an encouraging and positive work environment?

ANSWER GUIDE

Number of Yes Responses

13   Put this book down right now! Your workplace is perfect. Find something else to read.

10–12 Have a job for me? Sounds like a pretty good work environment.

7–9   You may have a negativity problem here. You better continue reading.

4–6   Getting very serious here. Extreme negativity. You need all the help you can get.

0–3   You are probably feeling totally negative at this time. Emergency help is on the way!

Appendix B

COMMONLY ASKED QUESTIONS ABOUT WORKPLACE NEGATIVITY

Here are some of the more common questions asked at both public and in-house seminars on how to manage workplace negativity.

1. *How do I motivate employees who have become negative because they have been passed over for promotion?*

If they were the best candidates and they were passed over, they probably have a right to feel negative. You need to be very supportive at this time and empathize with them. You do not want their negativity to lessen their work performance. You also have to be aware that they make try to make others feel their negativity.

In other cases, employees may believe they were the best candidates but in reality were not. One of the best things to do is to explain and give reasons why they were not ready for the promotion. Also, you should work with them to develop a career plan that contains specific work-related goals. In this way they can work on any of their performance gaps and be ready for the next opportunity for promotion.

2. *How do I manage my boss's negative attitude? His behaviors affect our attitude toward work.*

If you have a good relationship with your boss, you should give him or her some honest feedback. Make sure the feedback states how the boss's negativity is affecting the department's or the organization's goals. Try to make it a business issue and not only an interpersonal communication problem. If the boss is a tyrant or you are afraid to approach him or her, you may have to live with it.

If the behavior really gets bad and begins to seriously affect your performance, that of your coworkers, or your success within the organization, you need to speak to human resources or jump a level. This could be quite risky. You have to know your organization quite well before taking this drastic step.

3. *Other than money, what other things can be used to motivate my staff to keep them more positive?*

Providing them with interesting work, a fun environment, and positive feedback; establishing good relationships between them and their supervisors; and showing them that the organization is very loyal to them would reduce negativity and make most individuals much more positive.

4. *How can I prevent an employee from spreading negativity throughout the team?*

First you need to find out why the person is being negative. Ask her for the reasons or any problems that she may be experiencing. There may be many things you or the organization can do to stop her negativity if she has valid reasons for feeling negative. If that turns out not to be the case, you need to communicate to her that this type of behavior is unacceptable and discuss what you need for her to do instead.

5. *How do I keep a positive attitude when I do not respect my boss?*

This is quite challenging. Many studies have shown that the most important factor for happiness at work is one's relationship with his or her immediate supervisor. I suggest you focus more on your work and the results you are achieving and the furtherance of your career goals. Try to make those your focus at work. If you respect your work and other colleagues or others in leadership positions, the negative boss will have a less devastating effect on you.

6. *What can I do if organizational negativity stems from constant change?*

We cannot avoid change, and it is going to hit us at an even more rapid pace in the coming years. The best thing you can do is to discuss the need for the change before making a decision on whether to implement it. Then point out its benefits and get the people involved in implementing it. If you get a negative reaction to the proposed change, do not automatically blame the person for being resistant to change or frozen in his or her ways. Take a look at how you or the organization is handling the change process. That is where the problem often lies.

7. *How can I get the message across quickly that negativity will not be tolerated?*

The best thing you can do is to make it a criterion for performance for each staff member and include it in the performance review process. I also strongly suggest tying it into salary or bonus reviews. The staff member will quickly get the message that negativity is not tolerated. He or she will clearly see the direct connection between being negative and how it affects his or her review, salary increase, or promotional opportunities.

8. *How do I keep workplace negativity from seeping into my personal life?*

The best strategy is to try to separate work from the rest of your life. When you leave work each day, try to have other things planned and have other interests to take your mind off work. And if you can avoid it, try not to take work home with you. About 90 percent of the people who do never get to it anyway.

9. *How may I unconsciously be encouraging negativity?*

You may not even know it, but you may be using some negative words at work, or you may be putting down the company or some of its procedures or management decisions, or you may be demonstrating some negative body gestures or facial expressions, or your voice may have a negative tone. Most negative people are not aware that they are coming across as negative.

10. *How can we minimize the level of negativity in our organization?*

This is a very broad question, and each organization may have to strategize differently. Generally speaking, however, organizations need to identify why the negativity exists, come up with action plans for reducing or managing that negativity, and then reward people for changing, or hold them accountable if they do not.

11. *What can I do with my work group to prevent negativity before it starts?*

Constantly monitor them for any signs of negativity and address these signs as soon as you see them. Never give people the message that it is OK to be negative. Open channels for communication so you can be aware of any potential problems that may cause negative work group reactions. Also, build up the skills and commitment levels of each work group member. Finally, be a role model for the way you want your work group to behave and perform.

12. *How can I get myself to look at the cup as half full and not half empty?*

This is not easy, especially if you have been "programmed" over the years to see the negative side of things. The programmers in this case are family members, friends, workplaces, and school experiences. In a sense, they made us see the cup as half full or half empty.

It is up to us to change things. Begin to view yourself differently. Practice giving yourself positive self-talk or seeing the positive side to any situation. The more you say positive things to yourself and the more you see good where once only bad existed, the higher your self-esteem and self-concept become. It is our self-esteem and self-concept that influence whether we think negatively or in a more positive way.

13. *How do I eliminate negativity from long-term employees who are just waiting to retire?*

The trick is not to allow them to be waiting, while on the job, for retirement. Find new opportunities and challenges for them, continue to involve them, make them mentors, and so on. If they do not buy into these approaches, remind them of their job responsibilities and the standards of performance expected of them. It is never too late to hold someone accountable for doing what he or she is supposed to do.

14. *How can we identify hidden negativity?*

Hidden negativity occurs when individuals are not

feeling positive about where they work or what they do but for various reasons do not overtly demonstrate their negativity. They may not be expressing it for fear of retribution. In some work environments, feelings of any kind are not welcomed. This form of negativity is often found in organizations with an extremely strong leadership that does not accept any human frailties. Hidden negativity ultimately shows itself through increased turnover, high levels of stress, increased medical claims, and a lessening of quality. Anonymous organizational surveys will pick up on any hidden negativity.

15. *In a few sentences, describe what you mean by workplace negativity.*

Workplace negativity is an attitude that people have toward their work, bosses, colleagues, or customers. It causes conflicts and the lowering of morale, productivity, and profitability. Work environments that do not meet the staff's developmental or motivational needs or avoid confronting individual negative reactions allow workplace negativity to continue and flourish.

16. *How is negativity related to anger?*

Negativity is just one of the many ways in which we express our emotions. Anger is one of the stronger emotions. Many people have learned to express their anger by becoming negative. Other reactions to anger would be to yell, throw things, withdraw from the situation, curse, drink, or engage in sabotage. Healthier, more positive reactions to anger would be talking about how you are feeling, and trying to determine what triggers your anger and how to handle it in a more constructive way.

17. *How much do family and personal differences in upbringing influence negativity?*

These aspects of our histories affect us tremendously. The way we were raised and the people who raised us greatly influence our perception of the world and how we handle situations that do not go our way.

18. *Why are some people so positive while others are so negative?*

People learn to behave in different ways based on their role models, their experiences, and the type of behaviors for which they get rewarded. Many negative people get rewarded for behaving negatively. They get people's attention or approval. When this occurs, negative people continue to be negative. It may even become the norm of how to behave in organizations. If everyone around you is behaving in a negative way and you want to fit in and be part of the group, you will become negative as well.

19. *How do I keep a positive mindset around negative people?*

Try to remember that their negativity is not directed at you personally. Do not become defensive or attack them. Your doing so will make them even more negative. Focus on the positive things you have going for yourself at work and in your personal life. Make it a personal challenge to remain positive when you are surrounded by negativity.

20. *How do you keep employees positive in a downsizing environment?*

There are a few things you can do. First, do not drag out the process. Let people know as soon as possible if they are the ones to go. When this change process takes too long and people are not given the information about what is happening, negativity increases tremendously. Second, recognize that those who stay may become negative as well because they have lost people they were used to working with, and their job responsibilities might have changed. Be aware that they may be upset and give them the time to readjust. Third, actively help those being let go to find new positions in other organizations. This gives them a more positive attitude toward the company that has eliminated their jobs and sends a message to those who remain that the company is concerned about everyone's future.

21. *If being honest and telling the truth creates negativity, is it better to lie?*

Telling the truth is better. For example, if you have to introduce a new process within your group that you disagree with and know that your group also disagrees with, hiding your view from the group is the lie. When people eventually find out the truth about what you originally thought (which happens nine out of ten times), they are likely to become even more negative about this process. Be clear, however, that as a team player you support the decision.

22. *Does conflict always create negativity?*

Workplace conflict has many positive aspects. It forces people to discuss issues that they normally would not. As a result of conflict, new ideas or new approaches to solving problems emerge. It is definitely positive when staff is in conflict about how to make a service or product better. When people are so concerned about pleasing the customer and arguing about how to do it, a company or organization cannot ask for a more positive situation.

Conflict can be a negative, however. Communication can stop, people put down their colleagues or bosses, and morale and productivity decrease.

23. *The members of my current project group are very negative. I have forgotten what it is like to work on a high-performing work group. How would I recognize one?*

A high-performing work group always knows its purpose. Its members rely on one another; there is open, honest communication; each member has a clear role and a set of responsibilities; and all members achieve their goals. They also enjoy working with one another.

24. *I have a work group that used to be very negative. After quite a struggle, I have turned around their attitude. What can I do to encourage them to continue their new ways?*

You can give the group positive feedback and let others in the organization know how well they are doing. You could also celebrate their success. Throw a party, take them out to dinner, or purchase some small gifts. A cash bonus or spot award would send a clear message that you appreciate their new behavior.

25. *What role should I as a work group member, not the leader or manager, play when a member of the group is being negative?*

Take the responsibility of speaking to your colleague about his or her behavior and how it is affecting the group's performance. Ideally this person will heed your advice and change his or her ways. Of course you might not always be able to turn around the person's behavior. In that case, you will have to speak to the group leader about it and have him or her address the issue.

Quite often I have found that work group members have much more of an influence on their colleagues' work behaviors than does the leader or manager. In fact, having team members evaluate, discipline, motivate, and coach one another is becoming quite popular in many organizations today.

26. *What is the best tactic for dealing with a negative colleague: reasoning, anger, joking about it, or ignoring it?*

Depending on the colleague and the way this person expresses his or her negativity, different tactics will work better. It is best to understand the person's work style and how he or she responds to feedback. Never ignore the behavior for more than a few days; this gives the person the impression that it is OK to be negative.

27. *What is the connection between home life and negativity on the job?*

Many people who have unpleasant personal lives or are going through a temporarily difficult time will often let these situations influence their work attitudes. We must recognize that this will happen and be understanding. We must remember that all members of our work group have a complicated life outside of work and that they have had to make adjustments to be able to be here. Nevertheless, when a staff member's personal problems constantly cause him or her to have a negative approach to work, that negativity must be addressed. Offer the person some help or counseling if necessary, but remind him or her that negativity cannot be expressed at work.

28. *When I am having a bad day at work, what can I do to relieve my stress so that I do not transmit my negative feelings to others?*

That you are aware of your negativity and are concerned about spreading it is the crucial first step. Most people in negative states of mind want to spread it to others. It is very refreshing to hear individuals who realize that they are negative and are trying not to influence others. I would suggest that you take a few deep breaths often throughout the day, buy yourself one of those stress-relieving balls and squeeze it, take short breaks to escape the stress of the day, go out to lunch, keep a mirror on your office wall so you can see your facial expressions, call a friend or family member who can cheer you up, or have a picture of your favorite place in the world as your screen saver.

29a. *How does one catch the negativity bug at work?*

As with any virus, a few things have to occur. You have to come into contact with the virus. In this case it is a person with a bad attitude. Then you have to be receptive to the virus. That is, there has to be a reason why you would be open to the negativity. Perhaps company profits are down, or you did not get that promotion, or the boss has chewed you out, or you are insecure about the impending reorganization. You now have the virus. But after a day or two you probably can shake it off, unless it becomes a permanent condition. It can become permanent or linger on if you keep getting exposed to it, if you are open to it (if your positive immunity is down), and if no one tries to help you treat it or if you cannot treat it on your own.

29b. *If a coworker has a negative attitude and is a constant complainer, for example, how do you judge whether he or she is harmless or a virus carrier?*

Anyone who has a negative communication style is a potential carrier. The only way your coworker can spread the virus is if other people are receptive to it. If other work group members have a positive attitude or can discount the behaviors of this complainer, they will not catch the virus. After many repeated contacts with this same person or other coworkers with negative habits, however, it will get harder and harder for them to fight off the virus.

30. *I work for a company that is doing quite well now. With increasing competition, however, I am worried about our future. One of our biggest barriers to success is the negativity that seems*

to exist within all areas of the organization. What can we do to eliminate negativity?

Trying to eliminate negativity is an exercise in futility. Negativity can never totally be eliminated. There will always be incidents to cause people, work groups, departments, or entire organizations to become negative. The job of the organization is to teach its staff and leaders how to manage negativity.

Appendix C: Case Study

SONDY INC.COM

Sondy Inc.com is an Internet provider start-up in New York City's Silicon Alley. After about nine months of operation, the negativity bug hit. This case study describes how Sondy is successfully fighting it off.

Even though Sondy is a small, fifty-five-person company, the same or similar principles that it is using to fight negativity can be applied to much larger organizations.

BACKGROUND INFORMATION

In December 1999, Tom Morgan and Bill Roddick, two MBA buddies from Princeton, created Sondy Inc.com. They had planned the business for about eighteen months, working out of Bill's SoHo apartment. Within the first two months of operation, their business grew to more than a million dollars in sales. As a result of this rapid growth, they hired additional staff at all levels, rented a large corporate office, and planned for future growth. Everything continued to go remarkably well for another few months. Their profits doubled. A couple of months later, however, they noticed that the mood among staff had changed. People were acting in a negative way. They were disagreeing with company directives, were pessimistic about future growth, and had lost their high energy levels. Fun and excitement disappeared from the office. To make matters worse, revenues began to slide. When the staff turnover rate reached approximately 18 percent, I was brought in to determine what was going wrong and to strategize on how to turn things around.

ASSESSMENT

I observed the organization in operation and interviewed most of the staff, including Tom and Bill, extensively. I also interviewed job candidates about their initial impressions of the organization and familiarized myself with the Internet provider business. Practically everyone with whom I spoke was quite candid. Tom and Bill were hoping for a quick turnaround.

FINDINGS

Based on my assessment of the industry and the internal goings on at Sondy, I came to the following conclusions about what was causing the sudden high levels of negativity and the resulting loss of sales and high turnover:

■ Sondy's administrative manager, Sheila, and receptionist, Alfonso, were spreading negativity around the office. Sheila, who had a long career in human resources, went around talking about how Tom and Bill did not know what they were doing and how much money they were making (which was not the case) and how the rest of the staff were underpaid compared with the employees of other Internet companies. She also seemed to hire support staff that was more interested in making a quick buck than in honing their skills or supporting the growth of Sondy. These new hires were also underqualified. I got the sense that Sheila wanted to maintain tight control over them. She was originally hired because neither Tom nor Bill knew anything about recruitment, interviewing, employment law, training and development, and so on. Her negative behavior influenced those around her. Many of the staff, especially those she hired, seemed to catch her negativity bug.

Alfonso, whom Sheila had hired, had a paralanguage problem. He was extremely loud on the phone and had a sarcastic, whiny voice. As a result of his behavior, both external and internal customers felt devalued. They interpreted Alfonso's behavior as negative, causing great harm to the company's image. All of the interview candidates with whom I spoke could not believe Alfonso's attitude either on the phone or when they met him in person on the day of their interview.

- Tom and Bill are great technicians. They seemed to know everything about the Internet provider business. However, they never developed their people skills or really thought about how important these skills were for managing others. They did not realize that constant communication as to what was happening, getting the staff's input, and allowing them to be part of the decision-making process were important. Additionally, they never thought about how daily major changes affected the staff. The bottom line is that neither had any prior organizational experience and never focused on the people side of developing a business.

- Along with Tom and Bill, the staff members hired to take on managerial roles as Sondy grew had no clue on how to manage others. They were highly demanding and accepted no excuses. They believed that their people were hired at good salaries and should do whatever it takes to get the job done, even if it meant giving up their personal lives for the company.

Staff also became negative when these managers were hired from the outside. They believed that Sondy had the talent and expertise right there. Additionally, all of the managers (there were five) were college buddies of Tom and Bill. This set up an environment of "Princeton" against us. Employees felt that if they had not gone to Princeton, they were considered outsiders.

Even though the staff were earning salaries comparable to those of their counterparts in other Internet provider companies, they were not receiving the external motivators so common in these other organizations. Tom and Bill's philosophy was to put the profits back into the business. This way, the company would grow, and the staff would eventually reap the benefits.

Most employees did not buy into this philosophy. They were not necessarily there for the long haul. They expected to be rewarded now if the company was doing well. They also believed that if Sondy hoped to get their loyalty, then it would have to demonstrate concern for its employees' well-being.

- Tom and Bill never established clear goals or performance standards for their managers. In turn, their managers followed suit. The lack of anyone at Sondy doing so resulted in unclear roles and responsibilities. I often got the sense that no one really knew exactly what he or she was supposed to be doing or what others were supposed to be doing. This led to a chaotic environment. It was as if Tom and Bill were still working only with each other. They rarely ventured out of their offices and never held staff meetings. They felt obliged to hire more people when profits soared in order to make even more profits. They just never figured out what to do with their people or how to organize them.

The combining factors of poor management at all levels, two strong negativists, an inappropriate reward system, hiring mistakes, and a lack of a communicated organizational direction led to an increase in negativity. The negativity then began to affect turnover, productivity, and morale, which in turn affected sales and profits.

ACTION PLAN

The strategies I devised for Sondy are currently being implemented. We decided to develop action plans to address all of the causes of workplace negativity identified. Tom and Bill wanted to engage in an all-out attack on negativity. I concurred with them, because if they did not, chances are that Sondy would soon be out of business.

1. CONFRONT INDIVIDUAL NEGATIVITY

Both Sheila's and Alfonso's negativity is being addressed by Tom and Bill. They have spoken to both staff members and have described to them in very specific terms how their current "attitude" needs to be changed. They monitor Sheila's and Alfonso's behavior on a daily basis and hold weekly coaching sessions with them. Both employees have been made aware of the consequences of noncompliance.

2. MANAGEMENT AND LEADERSHIP TRAINING

It was quite evident that Tom, Bill, and the other managers had never had any formalized training on how to lead others. They have just finished a five-day program on how to communicate, listen, give feedback, interview, and set goals, standards, and performance measurements. In a few weeks they will focus on motivating others, delegating and developing others, and coaching.

3. PROMOTE FROM WITHIN

A promote-from-within policy is now the norm at Sondy. When a position becomes available, it is first offered to any qualified staff member. Outside candidates will be considered only if no matches are found internally. Sondy now offers training programs that allow staff to develop skills so that they will be able to compete with outsiders for higher-level jobs.

Additionally, staff are encouraged to recommend skilled and motivated friends, family members, and other acquaintances for open positions. The staff member receives a finding bonus whenever he or she identifies someone who is hired and works out.

4. A REVISED REWARD SYSTEM

Staff will now be part of a profit-sharing plan. A certain percentage of profits (if there are any) will be distributed among staff on an annual basis as a bonus. Staff will also be paid for performance. That is, the better their semi-annual review, the more opportunity they have to get cash rewards. In addition, the managers will recognize individual and team efforts, and at their discretion, spot cash awards will be given.

The benefits package is currently under review. It was believed that it should be more competitive with similar companies. Sondy is willing to make the adjustments when the results of the study are received.

5. Managing Change

Bill and Tom and the other managers will be much more astute as to how they introduce and manage change. They are now aware of what makes change work and are ready and able to use their learning on a day-to-day basis. They understand the connection between not handling change well and the ensuing negative reactions of staff.

6. Changing Negative Norms into Positive Ones

A team of mangers at Sondy has identified several organizational norms associated with pride, management effectiveness, communication, and teamwork that are not serving Sondy well. They have established a very detailed action plan for changing each of these negative norms into a positive one. For example, one of the current norms is that Sondy cannot successfully compete in the long run with other Internet provider companies. The managers want the new norm to be that Sondy will be and is a developing player in the Internet provider arena.

RESULTS

1. CONFRONT INDIVIDUAL NEGATIVITY

Sheila has improved tremendously. She no longer criticizes management or their decisions. She is now recruiting for qualified staff who will show loyalty to the company. She even talks up Sondy as the place to be.

Alfonso has not made any progress. He still uses inappropriate language and vocal tones and expressions while communicating. He was offered a job with no customer contact within Sondy but refused. He was also offered outside counseling if he so desired. He refused that as well. He was sent to telephone and interpersonal skills training. But he has not changed much. He is currently on a discipline plan and has one more week to go before the final step of termination is taken. Sheila doubts if he will improve.

2. MANAGEMENT AND LEADERSHIP TRAINING

The first part of the training has gone very well, and the managers (including Bill and Tom) have really changed how they work with others, especially those reporting to them. They are much better communicators and setters of policies, procedures, and goals. Initial employee feedback indicates a near 180-degree change. The same reactions are hoped for after they finish the second part of their training.

3. PROMOTE FROM WITHIN

Already there have been two cases in which employees were promoted from within. They appear to be able to handle the jobs and are getting excellent reviews from their colleagues. One of the promotions was to the managerial level. Princeton has now been infiltrated! This policy has given staff the motivation to work hard and to stay at Sondy.

4. A Revised Reward System

The reward system is now in place, and a few people are just about to reap its benefits. One way to achieve a bonus is to make a sale of more than $20,000. Five such bonuses have been given out so far. Bill and Tom used to handle the big accounts. Now they are assigned to the sales team. The staff are also taking their semi-annual reviews much more seriously, because an excellent review could mean a salary increase. A poor review, on the other hand, could mean termination.

5. Managing Change

The staff at Sondy is now much less resistant to change. The managers have worked hard on making this happen. They now communicate the change early and always point out its reasons and benefits. They involve those whom the change will affect in deciding whether the change would be of value to Sondy. Recently, a few staff members disagreed with an impending change, and Tom and Bill backed down on it. Staff now owns the change as well as Tom and Bill and the other managers and takes responsibility for its success or failure. They no longer blame the company or the bosses when a change does not work out.

6. Changing Negative Norms into Positive Ones

Sondy has been able to transform many of its negative norms into positive ones by confronting negativity, providing management training, promoting from within, revising the reward system, and managing change more effectively. For example, the staff no longer believes that Sondy is not a good place to work or that it will not succeed as a new Internet provider. They talk the company up and are proud to be part of the team effort.

CONCLUSION

I am really amazed at how Sondy has become a much more positive place to work. This case study demonstrates that any environment, no matter how negative, can become more positive. Such a transformation takes a great deal of commitment, planning, and perseverance. Sondy is well on its way to eradicate negativity, but it still has some more work to do. It must continue to confront negativity whenever it arises. Management needs to be constantly reminded of what it takes to be an effective leader. Staff needs to feel important and believe that their contributions are significant. Promoting from within and rewarding employees are two of the best ways to promote this belief. Tom and Bill have seen the change that occurs when change is managed well.

Organizations can use many other strategies to fight negativity. The methods that worked well for Sondy may not work as well in other organizations. Each organization needs to develop its own plan of attack. Organizations do not have to tolerate negativity. There are ways to manage it.

INDEX

hidden, 167–168
impact of, 5–9
influencing factors, 9–15
internal causes of, 5
nature of, 3–5
pervasive, 81–92

and physiology, 15–16
strategies for handling, *see*
   quick fixes for negativity
and three c's, 9–15
as virus, vii, 4, 173
work style, 172